**A gift from**

## NDN BONUSES INCLUDE:

✓ Four Part Story Structure Scrivener Starter File
✓ Four Part Story Structure MS Word Starter File
✓ FREE and Bargain Book Marketing Submission Site List
✓ *Nine Day Novel: Self-Editing* Bonus Videos
✓ And much more!

### *Two ways to get instant access to the bonuses and more*

**ONE -** Simply enter your email on any of our free product pages at https://authorbasics.com/shop/ and click the "Download Now" button.

**TWO -** Avoid entering your email for each freebie you want by becoming a FREE member of Author Basics, our author training community, at https://authorbasics.com/join/
**THEN** Login at https://authorbasics.com/my-account/
**VISIT** the bonus blog category or https://authorbasics.com/shop/
**ENJOY** the freebies!

NINE DAY NOVEL

# WRITING

STEVE WINDSOR

Published by

Vixen

# VIXEN ink

## *NINE DAY NOVEL: WRITING!*

A VIXEN ink book/Published by arrangement with the author

(Printed Version)
ISBN-13: 978-1507742198
ISBN-10: 1507742193

## Dedication

*To you believing that you can and will write your novel!*

# Table of Contents

Title Page .................................................... iii

Copyright .................................................... iv

Dedication .................................................... vi

TABLE OF CONTENTS .................................................... vii

Foreword .................................................... viii

So You Want to Write a Novel? .................................................... 3

9 Days? Are you Crazy? .................................................... 15

Speed Start .................................................... 31

Day 1: Outlining For Speed .................................................... 47

Day 2: Setting the Hook .................................................... 71

Day 3: Impossible Decisions .................................................... 83

Day 4: Run For Your Life! .................................................... 95

Day 5: Figuring Things Out .................................................... 105

Day 6: Fight Back, Fail .................................................... 117

Day 7: Rip the Rug Out .................................................... 129

Day 8: Climax Battle .................................................... 149

Day 9: New Equilibrium .................................................... 161

Word Count .................................................... 171

Next Steps .................................................... 175

Author Bio .................................................... 179

Urgent Plea .................................................... 181

**Foreword by Lise Cartwright**

**Why Steve is Awesome!**
Ok, so he paid me to say that!

Not really, but seriously, Steve is my go-to guy when it comes to learning fiction story structure. I've always wanted to write fiction, but the thought of coming up with characters, a world they live in, taking them through trials and tribulations to arrive at some amazing ending—well, it's more than a little intimidating.

I've been harping at Steve to teach me how to write fiction for a while now. Because I have some great ideas and a few characters running around inside my head that I'd love to see come to fruition, but, and it's a big BUT, I have absolutely no idea where to start.

Sure, I've heard about the four-part story structure (Which, by-the-way, made no sense to me until Steve explained it!), and I've got a Pinterest board full of pins on how to write a scene, how to develop a theme, how to kill a character, blah, blah, blah. None of it really made sense to me.

Enter Steve and his amazingly crazy 'write a novel in nine days' concept. The guy's a machine! But it can be done—

I watch him do it all the time.

When we first chatted about how he would teach me fiction, a few Google Hangouts seemed like the way to go. But I'm a hands-on type a gal and I learn by doing, so I encouraged Steve to consider writing a non-fiction book.

I have read through this book several times and each time, I learn something new. My favorite part is the story that Steve weaves throughout the book as an example of the four-part story structure.

Seeing Steve come up with a story while writing this book made things click into place for me. I was able to literally 'see' the story take shape and it has helped immensely in my understanding of story structure and plot development.

After reading and re-reading Nine Day Novel several times, my next plan is to write a novella. I'm going to have NDN right beside me every step of the way as I do this.

And if I can do it, you can do it.

YOU, the person who can actually write stories, YOU, the person who has conversations with their characters, and YOU, the secret author dying to finish those novels you've had languishing around for years and years. YOU can do it.

With Steve's help, I guarantee you'll get that novel done, and done right. And did I mention fast? This book is a great motivator and my word counts are on the rise using the tips he relentlessly drives home in it.

So without further ado, turn the page and "go learn things," as Dwayne Pride (NCIS: New Orleans) always says.

*Lise Cartwright*
Best Selling Author and Fiction Virgin

# NINE DAY NOVEL: WRITING

# SO YOU WANT TO WRITE A NOVEL?

You know there's a novel inside you, a story you're just itching to tell! And you *know* you could tell it in a unique way and tantalizing style all your own.

**So, where's your book?**

You've taken the courses. You've read the books. You've listened to the gurus. And you're totally pumped up to write. You sit down at your laptop and stare at it, wondering, *How do I do this? What do I write about?*

Or maybe you get discouraged just *thinking* about how long it will take you to bring your masterpiece to life? I know I did.

**Who this book is for**

I wrote this book and the entire *Nine Day Novel* series for us newbie fiction authors or anyone who wanted to learn basic story structure. I also wrote it to show you that you can carve out time to write.

It won't be easy, but I've done it exactly as I describe in

this book and you can too . . . if you want it badly enough.

I'll walk you through easy-to-follow steps you can use to write an entertaining story, have more fun doing it, and ignite your fire for fiction storytelling. And I'll do that by helping you make more efficient use of the *second* scariest part about writing a full-length novel—the commitment of your precious time.

I cover what we authors are *most* afraid of in *Nine Day Novel: Authorphobia.*

**What's My Secret?**

**There's no method or secret. I write—that's my secret.**

But it's not a secret, really. Not one you couldn't use yourself anyway. However, I do have a mission that drives me, and I'll tell you about that as I go.

As a budding fiction author, I struggled with self-doubt, self-sabotage, and self-consciousness.

Those things almost stopped me from even beginning to write a novel, much less finishing it before so much time had passed that I forgot what my own story was about.

But after a lot of trial and error, I'm now more self-confident that I have a decent story before I ever start writing.

I'm more self-reliant while I write it and more self-assured that I can finish it . . . fast!

Are you sensing any kind of trend? That's a lot of "selfs."

## Here's What You Can Expect From This Book

If you're looking for "magic", "secret sauce" or all that "easy" that other authors have been telling you about. . . Yeah, that's not in here. Here be only common sense, practical, doable advice on how to work harder to write more, matey.

## The PC version?

Each chapter in this book gives you short, "how-to" answers to your questions and easy-to-follow "action steps" you can take after reading it.

I'll share the writing tools I use every day, the tips I wish I'd had before I ever started writing fiction novels, and the "tricks" you can use to write your own novels faster.

With a pound of your personal passion, a peck of purposeful process, and a pinch or two of powerful prose, you'll have a repeatable recipe to help you finish the novel that's been nagging you inside your head. And you'll get it done years before you'd ever be able to, staring at a blank screen until the inspiration struck you to write.

## Let's Set Some Expectations

I'm pretty no-nonsense about writing. At the end of the day I look in the "mirror" (my little word counter at the bottom of my screen) and it tells me I either hit the number I wanted to . . . or I didn't.

If I did, I ask myself if I could do a little bit more. Many nights, I fall asleep sitting on the couch with my head slumped down, holding my laptop.

If I don't hit my number—my writing goal for the day—I'm not above brewing another pot of coffee so I can get the job done.

Why? Because I'm a writer. I write. And there's no one else there to make sure that I do it each day.

Before I got serious, I had this romantic idea of what being an author would be like. No bosses hanging over my shoulder asking me for another TPS report, no angry two-hour commutes in the morning and afternoon. Only the glory of writing wondrous stories for millions of adoring fans to buy and enjoy as I got rich.

I had to laugh at myself as I wrote that last line, because it reminded me of a line I wrote in one of my very first books.

*"Hard work is the Darth Vader of success—you can't become Luke Skywalker, Jedi Master, without it."*

It's no different in writing, because though the "force" may be inside you to write—you may have the drive and ability —that doesn't mean that learning to wield that power will be easy. In fact, a true master realizes that it should *not* be easy and he or she will never learn all there is to call himself a master.

## If it was easy. . .

If writing a full-length novel were easy, there wouldn't be so many unfinished ones languishing inside the laptops of would-be authors around the world.

But I'm not going to let that happen to you. Your book is getting finished!

## What You'll Learn

That's enough motivational mumbo-jumbo. Here are the facts you'll get from this book.

It's a fact that you get out of anything just about exactly what you put into it. I'm not going to tell you any nonsense about working smarter—writing is hard work and you're going to have to spend time working hard at it. But that doesn't mean you can't become more efficient.

**Speed does not kill.**

You can and will get better by going faster by learning to use tools.

I'll introduce you to the writing tips and tools that I use to do just that.

- You'll learn about the mechanics of story-telling.
- You'll learn how to come up with a killer concept for your novel.
- How to design a story that entertains.
- How to satisfy an audience's need for resolution.
- You'll learn a little time "management" for really intense people. (My own brand of crazy focus.)
- You'll get tips on how I write more words, more often, and with better results than the old adage of "just write a little bit a day and pretty soon. . ."
- You'll be introduced to a method for structured storytelling that's as old as Aristotle, and anything but mechanical. Trust me, you'll never watch another movie the same way again.

And all that will help you do the most important thing any writer can do for their stories—finish what you start!

## The best part?

I'll show you how it can be done in less than 10 days. Yes, I'm serious.

## Here's How This Guide Works

This book is a tool. Use the parts that you like and that work for you, and don't use the other stuff. All of this works really well for me, but I'm not you.

You have something unique that I can never have—you have the way you tell *your* story. I don't have that.

## The "WISK" Section

I was going to make this area one of those pithy "Stephen King quotes about writing" sections. But what works for the master may not work for the student, so I originally was going to call this "If I Were Stephen King." Then I just went for it and called it "When I'm Stephen King." The acronym worked better anyway.

## The "What You'll Learn" Section

The beginning of each section starts with "What You'll Learn."

I hate having to dig through tons of fluff to find answers, so I'm not putting any in this book. This area will be the quick and dirty lesson that will be expanded inside the following section or chapter.

## The "Been There Done That" Section

This area will be one of those adorable little parables about how I made mistakes and learned from them and then vowed I would never make the same mistake again. Only I screwed up and did it again even though I knew I shouldn't have . . . la-la-la.

You get the idea.

I like these sections in books; they let me know that the author isn't full of . . . it. That they've—wait for it—been there, done that.

## The "Nail on the Head" Section

This area will be the point or message of the entire chapter. I'll deliver it as subtly and as succinctly as a hammer pounding an anvil, lest you wonder how the cover of this book relates to its content.

This whole book—any book for that matter—is opinion, so there's really no sense being cryptic about what I believe will help you the most in a chapter or section.

## The "Tips, Tools and Time" Section

This area will be helpful hints, pitfalls to avoid, and any other tidbits of information that are pertinent and useful to the point of the chapter.

And the tools section will be either the name of or link to a particular writing tool that we use at that chapter's stage in the novel-writing process.

## The "Action Steps" Section

During the "writing phase" chapters, we'll let you know the next steps to take after reading that chapter.

Some of them may be as simple as "Go write for four hours." But no matter what they are, they'll be related to that section and they'll be something that you can physically do to drive your novel forward.

## The "10k A Day Strategy" Section

No, this section is not about how much you'll get paid. That'll come after the hard work.

Every once in a while, I'll sprinkle on a little bonus of information for you. Some hardcore—yet doable if you want it bad enough—suggestion about how you can write a novel as fast as possible.

Get in your 5,000 to 10,000 words a day.

After a lot of feedback, blasting me for unrealistic daily word counts for part-timers and moonlighting authors, I've added a **5k-a-day section** to my insane word-count tactics.

The reality for many of us is that we haven't and can't quit our day jobs yet. But I'm still going to challenge you to write more than that "vanilla" 1,000 words a day advice.

At first, it'll seem delightfully painful. But the time tactics I use *can* help you carve out more time to write. Maybe not as much as I suggest, but I wrote this book to show you that it *is* possible to write your novel much faster than you imagined.

Hint: Writing is still hard work. There's no getting around putting your butt in a chair and tapping the keyboard.

I've used all of the "techniques" in this book to write, edit, or finish a book on my deadline.

**Barring some note from your doctor that you simply**

"cannot lift a literal finger to write today," you can use them too. Some are painful, some are difficult, and some may make you want to cry and/or yell at me. Don't.

## Affiliate Links

Throughout this book, you'll find links to books, author pages, and software. These are affiliate links and I make a little money if you buy something.

You can be assured that I've read every one of the books and found something useful in each of them. I've watched the movies and loved them. I've used the software (Scrivener) and can't write fast without it!

## BONUS

If you're a dabbler, a wisher, a wonderer, or a wanderer with your writing, your success—finishing novels and making money—will be . . . difficult.

Get on a mission to write and succeed at becoming an author . . . right now! Make a vow to yourself that you will invest your time, energy, and money in your stories. That decision will make the biggest difference in your future success.

Chuck Wendig, one of my favorite no-nonsense authors, wrote a blog post about "aspiring" authors. He tells you to stop "aspiring" and start writing, because wanting and wishing never made an author.

In fact, that blog post will get you in the proper mindset to read this book.

**DISCLAIMER**—Chuck is rated (R) because he really doesn't want to hear your cry-baby whining voice . . . and he uses a lot of profanity. You've been warned.

Read Chuck's article HERE.

# 9 DAYS? ARE YOU CRAZY?

**I'm not crazy. I'm just focused.**

I first came up with the idea for this book after writing what is arguably my best effort at creating a great story, as of the date of the publication of this book.

My third full-length novel—*FAITH*, seventh if you count the ones that languish on my laptop to be published or properly edited and republished—took me literally nine days to write.

This book is my "money where my mouth is" moment. And though, yes, I am crazy about writing fast, I haven't lost my mind in believing that *you* can write your novel in nine days, too. At the very least, I'm going to push you to do it faster.

**Will it be difficult**—will Darth Vader be there to scare you with his big red lightsaber? In a word . . . **yes**.

**Will** you be able to believe that you can do it? **Will** you be able to start it? **Will** you finish it? That . . . **will** be up to you—your "**will**."

Because the way I write isn't for everyone, but it can be used by anyone. **And where there's a will there's a way**. You bring your "will," I'll show you my way.

Let me define exactly what I mean by a nine-day novel.

## Reality Check

This isn't some book about how you can be living on your own private island in six months by only working four hours every month. I think you're probably smart enough not to believe that the woodcut word fairies are going to come down at night and do your writing for you.

And this isn't a book about how to get ghostwriters to work for you so you can sip Piña Coladas in Cancun while your Amazon sales skyrocket.

Ghostwriting strategies make people money, lots of money. However, they're marketers. They find a niche, outsource that pesky writing part, and market their product. That's fine, but I'm an author and so are you. *We* are going to write our own books. It's a . . . *novel* concept. [Dr. Evil puts little finger to corner of mouth.]

Sorry, sometimes I can't help myself.

## Everyone's Different

The strategies and tactics authors use to physically write their books are as numerous as novels themselves.

There's no catch-all, be-all piece of author advice that anyone can give you, including me, that will work for everyone. You have to find your own style, made up of conventional wisdom and what works for you and your situation.

All that being said, the rules for telling a great story have some pretty well-defined guidelines; the advice on how to get the words on the page is all over the map.

But by far, the "expert" advice we as authors are most inundated with is, "Write a little bit a day, every day. That's what you *have* to do."

There's no piece of writing advice I've found more difficult to wrap my will around than going slow and steady . . . on purpose.

**What does it mean to be an independent author?**

The strategy for independent authors has changed to a game of numbers, both in writing and number of books published. As such, I don't believe that writing faster is optional.

If I simply wrote slowly when I believed I had "time" to, I

might self-publish a book a year or at best a book a quarter.

Having started my writing career later in life, that pace would have me in the grave before I gained enough ground to make my writing dream a reality.

Because of that, I knew I had to write faster to catch up.

Not to mention the fact that as an independent author, you're going to have to do, or at least know *how* to do, everything.

Writing, editing (to an extent), formatting, self-publishing. . . Sure you can outsource all of it, but you'll still have to know how to communicate with freelancers and consultants. You'll have to know what you need in order to convey what you want from them.

**Turtle or hare? Which one are you?**

So with that hard-won knowledge in my mind, I simply shrugged off the "turtle wins the race" mentality and wrote as fast and as often and for as long a period of time as I could—or my wife could stand to be without me.

As it turns out, my wife can go without me for longer periods of time than I would've ever imagined [tongue in cheek].

Seriously, though. . .

My goal is to give you some of the wisdom and motivation I've gained through writing well over a million fiction words. Take my advice, and any you get about how you should write, with a grain of salt. **Sift out the advice that makes sense to you, use it, and throw out the rest.**

A word of caution. . .

**Don't say you lack time**. That's what people say who have better things to do than write.

## WISK (When I'm Stephen King)

"I love my TV. I'm just not speaking to it right now." - Steve Windsor

## What's in a Novel?

A novel—as defined by many different sources—is a story that contains a minimum of 40,000-50,000 words . . . "ish."

For our purposes, we'll use a nice, round, mathematically "friendly" number. You'll see why shortly.

50,000 words averages out to be around 200 pages long

if you count like Amazon does at roughly 250 words per page. However, most paperback novels average out to be between 300-375 pages long.

**360 pages—it's kind of a sweet spot.**

Around 85-90,000 words is long enough to be considered a full-length "novel" and short enough so that the average reader doesn't look at it and say, "I'll never be able to read all of that anytime soon," and thus decide not to even buy the book.

Oh sure, in actual printed books there are production costs and economies of scale to consider, then there's physical size and convenience of the book, font selection and size parameters that publishing houses use to adjust and hit that sweet spot. But to simplify things, the average paperback novel is around 300-400 pages long.

Don't believe me? Go check it out.

I actually stood in a Walmart and checked the page counts of every book they had in their thriller section, and almost every novel's page counts were between 300-400. (So when you go and do this yourself, because that's what we writers do, yes, there were a few that were 401, and George R.R. Martin's *Game of Throne* books are a crazy 700-plus pages, but those are the edges of the curve. We're splitting things right in the middle of the sweet spot.)

I did some more math—something you'll learn to do to get your mind past your fear of big word counts. Here's what I figured out:

There wasn't a novel in the group that didn't average out to about 250 words per page. (Believe me, I counted lines per page and words per line many times to check. I guess I'm a little freaky like that.) That put the actual average word counts at around 75,000-100,000 words.

I can feel you squirming in your skin just reading those numbers. That's okay, because I did the same thing before I learned to look at them differently, and found writing tools to create and manage those word counts more efficiently.

## What's in a Day?

Since this is a nine-day novel, first let's define what a "day" means . . . to me.

A day, by any other name, is 24 hours in the rotation of the Earth on its axis as it moves around the sun each year. From 12:01AM to 12:00 in the deep dark night. And a heck of a lot happens between those hours. Most of it can be pretty much considered the minutiae of life.

Ever heard the saying, "Life's what happens while you're making other plans"? That's exactly what a day is and how most of us treat most of the days we have.

Commuting, going to the grocery store, cooking meals, and the dreaded zoning out in front of the TV. All of these are how many of us spend a lot of our precious time.

So when I said, "We were going to learn some psychotic time management" at the beginning of this book, I wasn't kidding. We have to get some of that time back!

**I should call it time *attainment*,** because typing at a constant rate with a constant overall word count goal means that no matter how much "smarter" you work, a 90,000-word novel at an average typing speed of 1,000 words per hour will take you 90 hours to complete.

Life hacks or not, you have to find 90 hours, or increase your typing efficiency. And the only way to do that is to type more words, so you still need the 90 in the first place. See where I'm going with this?

**An Author's Day**

In this book, and as it pertains to writing your novel, we're going to define a day as "the 10 hours during the course of a 24-hour period in which you would have been otherwise engaged in either working your standard 50-hour work week, or running around inefficiently using your day, getting distracted and dealing with life."

**A big part of this book is not necessarily learning to manage your time better; it's learning to take back the time you're letting slip through your fingers.**

I told you—common sense, practical advice only. And whether you like it or not, writing a novel takes—T. I. M. E. —a little acronym I just made up as I wrote that.

### *Time Invested Means Everything*

We'll talk about where you can find that investment later. Right now, here's what's coming—the next nine days!

### A High-Level Look at Days 1-9

**Day 1** - Killer Concept Creation - Novel Ideas - Outlining overview.

**Day 2** - Hook, Line and Sinker - How to start a novel that pulls in your audience.

**Day 3** - Scene, Setting and Seduction - How to make your reader care enough to keep reading.

**Day 4** - Retreat, Regroup, Run - How to write the dreaded middle pages of your novel.

**Day 5** - Halfway There - Figure out what you're really up against. You and your hero are halfway to the finish line!

**Day 6** - Fight Back and Fail - Conflict and struggle are the essence of your "story."

**Day 7** - Ripping the Rug Out - Just when you thought you were out, you get pulled back in. Your hero's world changes completely . . . again. Yours too.

**Day 8** - Climax - Why every story you've ever read or watched has a final battle scene.

**Day 9** - Dawn of a New Day - You and your hero have changed your world(s) . . . forever.

**Time Management and Work Ethic**

I alluded to this earlier in this chapter, but it warrants repeating.

Malcolm Gladwell, in his book *Outliers*, came up with an over-quoted rule pertaining to becoming an expert in any field after 10,000 hours. It may or may not be completely true, as I believe that different people learn and become proficient at different paces.

I think what he was really trying to say is that all else

being equal—skill and talent—anyone could learn to be an "expert" in 10,000 focused and fiercely attentive hours dedicated to becoming so.

I want to break that down for you, as I believe it pertains to writers, budding authors, or otherwise "experts" in writing. Given a pace of 1,000 words typed in an hour, according to Gladwell, it would take the average talented writer 10,000,000 words—that's a big fat "10M"—to become an "expert" in his 10,000-hour rule. And that breaks down to five full years at the 2,000-hour standard work year.

Now, if that were true, there would be very, very few successful authors out there.

So, let's put a more practical point on the 10,000-hour "rule" for us authors.

After struggling with half-starts, half-hearted efforts, and what couldn't even be called half-successes in writing novels, I finally settled on a variation to the 10,000-hour rule that I'm pretty comfortable with. Not ecstatic. I said comfortable. . .

**The 1,000,000-Word Rule. Or "1M."**

It takes me about one hour to write 1,000 words. At that pace, I reasoned, it would take me about 1,000 hours—

roughly half a "normal" work year—to get pretty good at writing fiction novels.

And low and behold, here I am, roughly 1,000 hours and 1M-plus words into it, and I'm pretty darned familiar with the concepts, work ethic, dedication, storytelling skills, and tools necessary to call myself—it's tough to call one-self an expert, but I'll settle for pretty good and on my way to being better.

My latest novel flew from my fingertips in less than nine full days . . . in a row. It's an 85,000-word . . . page-turner I'm told, and represents just about my 1.1 millionth written fiction word. More importantly, it has changed me from being a wishing-for-success writer to an author-on-a-mission, well on my way toward achieving my goals.

So, there's the math. Seems scary in the beginning—I know I was intimidated when I started my first sentence. But once you realize that you can type those words, it becomes less scary and more real.

## Time Management for Authors

So, where will you get the time that it's going to take to put in those 1,000 hours, especially if you already have a job, life, wife, husband, home, family, friends, and/or future to worry about?

I'll let you in on a little secret—you're wasting that time already . . . every single day.

Some of that time you can get back without giving up too much to do it, and some of it you'll have to sacrifice something. But it can be done, and nothing I ask you to do in this book will be life-threatening, just life-altering.

Okay, maybe the motel thing (that's foreshadowing—you'll find out later).

## The Inspiration for This Book

I wrote *FAITH*, the third installment in my *Fallen series* of religious thrillers, during my daughters' Christmas vacation.

I put in 85,000 words between four family Christmas parties (my wife's Italian Catholic, go figure) and a New Year's party. At the same time, I had to find entertainment for my six and eight-year-old daughters, and work with my wife to finish moving into an apartment we had only been in for less than a month. How did I do that?

**Easy, I wrote.**

- Instead of watching movies at night, I wrote.
- Instead of going to bed when everyone else did, I stayed up and I wrote.

- Instead of sleeping in late, I got up and . . . I wrote.
- Instead of surfing the Internet and posting on Facebook, I wrote.
- Instead of answering the tons of emails I get each day, I wrote.
- Instead of editing as I went, I just wrote . . . more.
- Instead of a one-hour meal, I got a slice of toast and a cup of coffee and I wrote.
- Instead of working out, I wrote.
- Instead of making an excuse to myself why I didn't, or couldn't, or wouldn't . . . I simply wrote.

And as I told you before, if I didn't hit my goal, I slapped myself across the face with some coffee and . . . you guessed it, I wrote.

**You gotta walk the talk!**

I won't deny that I can get maniacal when I get the right focus, but I know that's what it takes. And once you get in the fiction writing "zone," I don't like coming out unless a fire threatens to burn down the building. And even then, I want to remember to drag my laptop out with me. Don't want to lose all that hard work, do I?

But something in your life has to suffer, right? I mean, something has to give, because there are only so many hours in a day . . . right?

Sure—absolutely—I gave up chit-chat, and watching reality show actors dance with unknown dance instructors on TV, and I gave up letting my cell phone rule my life for a few days, and I gave up some sleep, and I gave up meeting my wife for . . . okay, you can only give up so much.

But you know what was the most important thing I gave up? The thing that the little critic voice inside my head missed the most? Can you guess?

**I gave up my excuses.**

No more justifying why I wasn't making money on Amazon, no more complaining about having to write another book right after I just finished two of them in three months, and no more whining about writing while everyone else was doing something more "fun."

But despite the will to carve out the physical hours and time to write, the one most important thing about the process I'd developed prior to writing *FAITH* was . . . I knew exactly **what** I **needed to write** . . . **before I wrote it**.

And that's what the rest of this book is about—structure!

## Action Items:

- Cut out some TV and write for that two hours instead. Give it a try—it won't kill you.
- Stop answering every phone call as if the Pope is calling.
- Let your email pile up for a few days, or better yet, select all and delete it. (I know, I know—you keep everything in there. But I tried it once, I'm still alive and the email is still coming.)
- Block out some time, go to a coffee shop, turn off your cell phone, and get ready to write your novel!
- Our daily word goal for "Day" 1 is 5,000-10,000.
- So block out the time: 5-10 hours.

# SPEED START

**WISK**

*"Speed kills? Whoever told you that crap?"* - Steve Windsor

**What You'll Learn**

If you're like me, you like things fast. When I buy a how-to book like this one, I pay $2.99, or $3.99, or even $47.99, so I can save time. I want to skip a direct coaching session with someone who's already climbed the mountain that I have to.

Enduring a one-hour video opt-in squeeze page so I can listen to something I may already know, then have to wait a week for the "meat" webinar in order to find that out, is a colossal waste of writing time. I wanna skip to the good stuff—get the message and the method we can use and apply right now!

And $2.99 is totally worth getting the one or two strategy-altering tidbits that just about every how-to book contains.

So in this chapter I'm just going to put all the high-level meat on the table and let you gobble it up as fast as you can.

Once again, all books—opinion. Here's mine . . . based on years and hundreds of thousands of words, of course.

**A day by any other name. . .**

When I'm struggling, my word count is down around 250-500 per hour, but once I get my creative engine revved up, and I'm sure you'll find this too, I can push, tap, punch my keyboard about 1,000-1,500 words an hour.

That author "zone" is where you want to be, because then you simply chase your characters through their story with your fingers. You don't have to coax them into acting.

You'll see what I mean later, but that's exactly why I don't like the ever-present advice of writing a little bit a day. It's hard to get myself immersed in my characters' worlds fast enough to make one hour of writing an efficient use of my time.

Don't get me wrong, I'll still do it when I have a free hour, or even fifteen minutes, but I find myself just getting up to speed when the deadline in my way slams the brakes on my creative mind. All that hard work pedaling up the creativity hill just to turn around when you're almost ready to coast down the other side. It sucks.

So a writing work day in my world is a concerted and focused 10 hours. Once I accepted that, then math and time start working for me.

I don't care if you write your novel in nine 10-hour days, 18 five-hour days; or four-point-five 20-hour days; nine days equals 90 hours at 1,000 words an hour average. And that's a 90,000-word, 360-page, sweet-spot novel.

## Blocking out time

If there's one key thing that I've practiced, read about from other authors, and focused my mind on creating, it's that there's no substitute for big blocks of uninterrupted time.

I'm not talking about one hour here and there, as you've been told to do by anyone and everyone. I consider two hours the minimum amount of time I need to put in some good writing word count. I'd recommend four straight hours as being better.

I regularly do my best—most productive and creative— work in 12-14-hour marathon sprints inside a coffeehouse from 5:00 AM to 7:00 PM, stopping only to get a caffeine refill.

If you have to leave for work at 7, get up at 5. If you come home from work at 7, grab a snack and write until 11. If you have kids . . . and I'm not letting you off the hook for this age-old excuse, because I have two daughters and I'm their "mother."

So if you do have kids, and you're a stay-at-home mom, dad, or grandma, or other, just wait until they go to bed at 8 or 9 and then write until 1:00 AM if you have to.

**Here's the good news**

When you're going to write a book as fast as we are, guess what, we get 48 "free" hours on the weekend to hammer out words. I bet you could get three of your nine days in right there, with nine hours a night left over to lounge in bed.

But Darth, I've had a hard week at work and my kids are driving me nut—go write! Writing is as relaxing and therapeutic, not to mention more rewarding, as TV is. And somehow we find time to do that for an average of four hours a day!

That's insane! You could finish a 90,000-word novel every 22.5 days by not watching TV.

I've done plenty of weekends where my wife took our daughters all day and I put out 25-30,000 words. And afterward, we all went out to dinner to celebrate. And you know what, I was exhausted as hell on Monday morning, but even happier that I wrote a third of my novel's draft in two days!

You have time; you're just not using it effectively.

Turn off your TV and electronic devices and let's go use some of it to write!

## Nail on the Head

Unless you physically put words into your computer, there will be nothing to edit, thus no novel or story will ever come to life from the most creative depths of your mind. Worrying about what those words look like as you go just delays the process.

I decided to really test this theory one morning, and being the aggressive sort of personality that I am, I decided that I was going to *really* test it.

I set my alarm for 4:30 AM, woke up, failed to brush my teeth or take a shower, drove to and sat outside in my car until my local Internet coffeehouse opened up. I got a coffee, put my butt in a chair in the corner, and I wrote . . . for 15 hours.

When I was finished, I had over 15,000 words to one of my first novels and I felt awesome. Well, figuratively I felt awesome inside, because I'd failed to eat or drink anything all day and when I stood up I got dizzy and fell back into my chair.

My back hurt, my butt hurt and my vision was blurry, but I had 15,000 words that no one else did and no one could take away from me. And . . . I recovered from the lack of food and water. I didn't die.

**If you get nothing else from this book, take away this: You have to type**.

The logic seems simple enough, but I've seen time and again where writers wonder why they aren't making any progress, myself included.

There's simply no better indicator of a writer's commitment to themselves than word count. And you get that while your proverbial "ass" is perched tight in a chair, couch, airplane seat, or bed.

I'm not above telling you that I've been so engrossed in writing something that I took my laptop to the toilet with me and typed.

## Scrivener: The ONLY Writing Tool

Before you type another sentence in the dreaded Microsoft Word, stop right now and go buy Scrivener.

As of this writing, it's only $45. (Of course I'm an affiliate —I LOVE this software!)

Learn to use it. I read *Scrivener for Dummies*. It was pretty good, but Scrivener is one of those programs you have to start using and learn as you go.

Once you get into it, the learning curve is no more difficult than when you first saw all of the knobs and dials in Word. And Scrivener has the advantage of being insanely useful to self-published authors, instead of a pain in the ass.

Later in this book, I'll give you a free Scrivener template of the story structure we'll discuss for our nine day novel. This one bonus alone will save you so much time, not only in creating the folders and documents for the Four Part Story Structure (4PSS), but the descriptions of exactly what you need to put in each one will save you tons of writing time.

**Creating a Killer Concept**

Coming up with a killer concept is arguably as important as writing a great story.

So what is it?

Simply put, something that no one has thought of before that would arguably make a cool story. Because high concept is a little bit like love—it's hard to explain it unless your in it.

"Killer concept" or high concept could be practically stated as a new and/or unexpected twist on a great old story.

**Example:**
My kids love the movie *Maleficent*. It's the story of Sleeping Beauty as told through the perception of the evil villain of the original story. They twist the plot so that she's neither villain nor hero, but a little bit of both. It makes for an excellent example of a killer concept—a new twist on a tried-and-true story.

**What if. . .?**

The best tool you can use to help you develop a killer concept is to ask yourself "What if?" and let your mind go wherever it wants to. That's how killer concepts come to life.

What if a spaceship full of miners absentmindedly brought a carnivorous alien back on board and it ate nearly every one of them? - *Alien*

What if the woman who survived that horror story was asked to go back and help an entire colony of people from more of those monsters, and then she ended up saving a little girl who was the only survivor? - *Aliens*

What if *that* woman survived only to find out that she was impregnated by one of the monsters and it was going to eventually, inevitably, eat through her stomach and kill her while the other ones attacked and killed everyone around her? What would she do? - *Alien 3*

What if, 200 years later, that woman figures out that she was cloned so she could be used to help scientists figure out how to use an entire pack of those carnivorous aliens as weapons? - *Alien Resurrection*

What if the priest who you thought was a bumbling, boozing blasphemer turned out to be a Shandian warrior for the Word, helping to carry out a plot as old as time itself in order to overthrow God and save the eternities from damnation? - My novel, *FAITH*.

Great stories all start with an author who asks him or herself, "What if?" And one man/woman or genre's killer concept is another's crap.

Take a look at some classic genres and ask yourself, "What if I mashed them together?"

**Western meets Sci-fi?**

What if a cowboy woke up in the desert with a weird wrist-cuff on, but he had amnesia? And then he got arrested in town because he was actually an outlaw. And what if just as he was being sent to the territorial marshall for trial, alien spaceships came down, blew the hell out of the place and kidnapped half the townspeople?

And what if during that raid, the cowboy's mysterious wrist-cuff activated and he blew one of the spaceships out of the sky? - *Cowboys and Aliens* Harrison Ford and Daniel Craig

Get creative, but don't get terrified, because one man's killer concept, is another's . . . crap.

**Getting Started**

Once you've familiarized yourself with the basics of the Scrivener Binder (outline window on the left) and the Editor (document writing window in the middle), and learned how to create folders (chapters) and documents (your novel's individual scenes), and worked your way through a killer concept, here's what this book is going to help you put in them.

If you're still in Microsoft Word, blaze forward—you can do everything in this book!

**Four Part Story Structure - 4PSS**

The 4PSS is as old as Aristotle and still used today in the majority of fiction novels. I'm not even going to debate its merits or alternatives here. The thing works, many authors use it—knowingly or not—and in the interests of speed and efficiency, I suggest you do too.

Abandon the 4PSS later if you want, but learning to tell a good story requires its elements.

The 4PSS takes your hero/story from a place of understanding to a state of confusion and then loss and then triumph and then understanding again. And that's done with conflict.

Conflict is great storytelling. If nothing happens to your hero . . . well, then nothing happens.

Learn structure and conflict. Here's the master. . .

## Story Engineering

You can put this book down and go buy Larry Brooks' *Story Engineering* for a long, in-depth analysis of the elements of story structure if you want to go deeper.

Not only does he outline 4PSS in depth and detail, but he has a similar writing voice to my own: "Do what I tell you and I may let you write 9,000 words instead of 10,000 tomorrow." I love him for that!

Dare I call him . . . Darth Brooks? [Dr. Evil—pinky to mouth again]

**I like a little juvenile humor to break up the monotony of learning, don't you?**

Ahem, here's what the 4PSS consists of at a high level. I've broken the four parts into two parts each to map to our writing schedule for *Nine Day Novel*.

You get one day to warm up and get your story concept/outline clear, and then two days for each section in the 4PSS.

It's not so tough. Stop crying.

**Mapping Our Days to the 4PSS**

**Day 1** - (10 hours) Brainstorm, killer concept creation, overlay your story onto the four part story structure's elements.

**Day 2** - PART 1 (5,000-10,000 words) **Hook - Opening scenes**, grab the reader with some exciting initial event, establish the hero and the stakes for success or failure.

**Day 3** - PART 1 (5,000-10,000 words) **Setup - Foreshad-**

**ow coming events**, set up the inciting incident, first plot point—inciting incident—hero has to choose.

**Day 4** - PART 2 (5,000-10,000 words) Reaction to the first plot point. **Retreat, regroup, run away!** Doomed attempt to take action.

**The flailing hero.**

In this section the hero fears for his/her life, maybe fights back a little, add a dash of fornicating to try and take the fear away, and you have about 90% of the stories ever written.

**Day 5** - PART 2 (5,000-10,000 words) Halfway There! - Hint at an evil hidden force against your hero. At the end of this section, the hero **figures out what they're up against** at the very physical middle of the book—page 200-ish. You and your hero are halfway to the end!

**Day 6** - PART 3 (5,000-10,000 words) **Fight Back and Fail?** - Reaction to midpoint of figuring out the threat. Hero takes matters into his own hands and fights back against the now—he thinks—known villain. Hint at the hidden evil force again.

**Day 7** - PART 3 (5,000-10,000 words) **Ripping the Rug Out!** - Just when you thought you were almost there, your hero's world changes completely. World changes again and what hero thought is not actually true. Second plot point at the end of this section. Start the ticking clock.

**Day 8** - PART 4 (5,000-10,000 words) **Climax!** - Hero accepts reality of his/her situation. The final battle scene against the evil force. Win and live, or die a martyr for a cause.

**Day 9** - PART 4 (5,000-10,000 words) **Dawn of a New Day—New Equilibrium.** You and your hero have changed your world(s) . . . forever. In the case of a trilogy or series, this is where a cliffhanger will go. Some unforeseen, but foreshadowed, threat that continues the hero's quest.

After filling in those parts and sections, you should have a 40,000 to 80,000-word novel rough draft. I know I said 50,000, but trust me, everything expands in editing.

**FREE 4PSS Template**

Still struggling with that scary Scrivener part? Staring at the Scrivener Binder, wondering what to do next? Wish there was some way to speed up the process of creating the Four Part Story Structure folders, scenes and outline?

I created a **Scrivener starter file** of the parts, scenes, and story milestones that make up the **Four Part Story Structure** to help you out.

You can **drag and drop the top-level folder** into an empty Scrivener project file, or one you're already working on, and then use it to "fill in the blanks" and outline your novel. Or you can simply open it fresh, and save it as your story. (It's not really a template, it's a full .scriv project starter file.)

It's pretty handy when you're first starting out in Scrivener.

Get my free, Four Part Story Structure, Scrivener Starter File Now!

**What You Need to Know to Start**

Before we go any farther, I want to make sure you have the tools you need:

- Scrivener - You've downloaded and installed Scrivener.
- 4PSS - You've read through and have a basic understanding of the Four Part Story Structure.
- 4PSS Starter File - You've downloaded and opened the 4PSS story structure Scrivener starter file from the previous section.
- You're committed to writing your novel in the fastest way possible!

If you've done all that, let's go to the next section!

**NOTE:**

There's a 4PSS MS Word .doc file in the same location as the Scrivener 4PSS starter file above.

**Tips, Tools and Time**

You have to block off time to give your inner creative genius the opportunity to exercise its muscles—to write. Schedule this time with yourself on your calendar if you have to, but don't let anything cancel it.

**Scrivener, Scrivener, Scrivener!** It has built-in word count goal-setting, tracking and calculating features that make keeping track of your progress fun and easy.

Track your words per hour each time you write to figure out your efficiency. TOTAL WORDS/HOURS.

**Word count is your gas mileage,** and it will help you figure out how long it will take you to finish a novel and how many hours you need to dedicate to it.

# DAY 1: OUTLINING FOR SPEED

**WISK**

*"Write what you're afraid to say. You'll get into more trouble."* - Steve Windsor

**What You'll Learn**

In this chapter, you'll learn how to:

- Come up with a killer concept for your story.
- Choose a title that jumps off the page.
- Outline your novel using the Four Part Story Structure.

**Been There, Done That**

When I sat down to write my first novel, I had no idea what I was doing and no idea where to go to find help. So I actually went to the store, bought a copy of *Buried Prey* by John Sandford . . . and I read it.

But I didn't just read it, I analyzed it as I read.

I looked at how the author started chapters, how long the book was, how exposition was intertwined with dialogue, what characters said, and how the book's dialogue was punctuated. And then . . . I sat down and I started writing.

And my first book . . . sucked.

But I wrote that book to prove to myself that I could put that many words down on paper.

In the process, I found out that I loved the writing!

**Nail on the Head**

Concept, Mind Map & Brainstorm

Word count is important in the beginning of any writing career—you must write to improve. But eventually, quickly, before word count can grind you to success, you have to know what to write about. This is where brainstorming a killer concept comes in, and then outlining that concept with the Four Part Story Structure.

Knowing *what* to write helps you write faster.

So before you shift into high gear and start pumping out the words in your novel, we're going to have to come up with a killer concept—something that will at least raise an eyebrow if not blow someone's socks off!

**Brainstorm High Concept Idea**

## Mind Mapping

Some authors swear by this method. It's a formalized and physical way of brainstorming ideas and then organizing your thoughts, coupled with using visual representations and images to use all the parts of your creative mind.

You start off with an idea of a story you might like to tell and then start jotting down any ideas, drawings, or imagery that pops into your head around that idea.

Start with blank pieces of paper or a whiteboard or three-by-five cards, and get down your ideas as they occur to you until some themes start to take shape.

The theory is that a common thread will emerge. One you never would have thought of had you not gotten all of your ideas out and together in one place.

I've never had any trouble coming up with ideas, though, and this method has sometimes left me more confused than when I started, so I usually do this right inside Scrivener by creating new documents for each idea I get.

But I have an even better way to spur your imagination, especially if you're experiencing writer's "block."

**10 Things I Hate. . .**

I read an article once. . . I can't find it, I tried, so if you call BS on me, I have no defense. But I read it, and it was about an author giving a class about brainstorming ideas on what subjects the students should focus on in their writing. He asked everyone in the class to write down a paragraph about 10 things they absolutely loved.

The entire auditorium sat for five minutes and not one of them could get a complete list of 10. So the author changed his tactics and asked them to write about 10 things they absolutely hated.

The entire hall silenced to scribbling and scratching in their notepads and at the end of their five minutes, many had more than 10 and far more creative ideas on things that they could write about.

If you can't brainstorm with "what if," then ask yourself **what 10 things do you hate that you would change if you could?** How would you change them?

**Ideas are everywhere.**

Once, while Stephen King was out for a walk. At a bend of the road, he saw a sign: Caution: Children. He suddenly imagined "two dead girls holding hands like paper dolls." The image stuck in his mind. And that sparked an idea for a book.

Watch the news, listen when you're in a coffeehouse, pay attention to the real world around you.

**Truth really *is* stranger than fiction.**

Recently, the San Francisco police recovered a suspicious suitcase. When they opened it, they found a dismembered body inside.

If you're a mystery, horror, crime drama or any other kind of genre, there's a concept for a story in there.

Maybe instead of one body, it was parts from ten, and the police had to set out to not only find the killer, but also figure out who the victims were . . . across the entire world. Then ask "what if." What if the police couldn't identify one of those body parts? And when they finally figured it out, it led them to a shocking discovery about the government trying to create alien-human hybrid cyborgs!

**Think the unthinkable.**

Writing fiction is about saying, discussing and taking to the extreme what no one wants to talk about or imagine or hope for in real life. Whatever you always wanted to say, but didn't have the courage to, write it.

**Pick a Killer Title**

There are all kinds of theories and schools of thought about what makes a good fiction title. However, most of those are only valid after the fact. Meaning, once a book is popular, it's easy to say why its title is so awesome.

*Harry Potter* is an awesome book name, not because *it* was an awesome name for a book series before it was written, but because now, after the millions have sold, *Harry Potter* is de facto an awesome name for a series of books about a young wizard.

Don't be afraid to experiment with titles. Run them by your friends, put them on your Facebook fan page—see what people like. But don't distrust yourself.

**Try an alliteration.**

I like alliterations. I feel like they stick in people's minds better. Hence the title of this book, *Nine Day Novel,* lends itself to a lot of "stickiness." NDN, 9DN, Nine Day Novel.

Whether it works remains to be seen, as the only measure of a really good title is how well a book sells. You won't know that until later.

**Amazon Titles**

On the other hand . . . the way people find titles and books is the same way they use Google on the Internet.

Amazon searches will give you a great reference on how you can name your books to put them in front of what people are already looking for. However, don't just name your book using a keyword.

Use something in the main title that's pertinent and relates to your book, then use a subtitle or descriptor phrase to get your book in front of Amazon search eyeballs.

My Book, *JUMP: A Futuristic Fantasy*, has some ugly keyword stuffing to get it in front of eyeballs, but the word "Jump" has a lot of meaning throughout the entire book and series.

All of the angel names in *The Fallen* series have special meanings—their names are shortened descriptions of them—so the main titles work well. *JUMP, FURY, FAITH, HOLE, DOGG, BURN, LIVED, LIFE, RAIN*, and *SALVATION* are all angels on a mission to save eternity. They are mean, nasty, sarcastic, and their names "fit" them.

However you name your book(s), go take a look at the Kindle category of similar books like yours and see how they're doing it. Find the best sellers, emulate, but don't copy them.

A great resource to use is www.yasiv.com. Enter in the name of the best-selling book or author from Amazon, and you'll see all the other books that customers also bought. These are also books you should be looking at too.

Many great titles hint.

*Twilight*—A love story with vampires and werewolves.

*Fifty Shades of Grey*—I don't even wanna go there.

**Fill in the Blanks**

To help you write your outline, I've turned each scene inside the 4PSS outline above into a question you can answer about your story. Fill in each of them and you'll have a rough outline for where you'll begin writing each scene/section of your story.

**PART 1 - SETUP**
Scene, Setting, Stakes

- Where do the opening scenes in your story take place?
- What's the mood, weather, feel of that place?
- What's your unexpected event to hook your reader early on?
- What thing will your hero see that will come back to haunt him/her later?
- What reaction does your hero have to the

hook incident?

- What would your hero do if faced with a moral decision that would harm him/her either way?
- What's your first plot point—inciting incident? The spur to the hero's quest?
- What will happen if your hero doesn't undertake the quest?

## PART 2 - REACTION

Retreat, Run, Regroup, Understand

- In this section the hero runs for his life.
- What is stronger than your hero's earlier want or desire that would make him/her flee in terror to save him/herself?
- What action will your hero take that will be ineffective in helping him/her?
- What is the evil force that may not be fully known to your hero?
- What is your hero's reaction to the hint at this evil force?
- How will you lead your hero to understand what he/she is up against?
- At the midpoint of your story, what revelation will the hero have?
- What will metaphorically, physically or spiritually "die" in your hero at the midpoint?

## PART 3 - PROACTION

Fight back and fail

- How will your hero react and fail to address the midpoint revelation?
- How will you hint at the evil force against the hero again?
- How will your hero react to that second pinch point?
- Will you have a pre-second plot point lull? Give your reader a little secret?
- How will you lead your hero up to the world changing completely again at the Second Plot Point?
- What Second Plot Point/revelation will your hero have that will allow him/her to finally understand how to defeat the evil?
- What impending event is looming—what clock is ticking? How long does your hero have to fix everything?

## PART 4 - RESOLUTION

Climax Battle Scene. In this section the outmatched hero fights the bad guy/gal and wins or is martyred.

- How will you show your hero accepting what he/she has to do to win?
- How/where will your final battle play out?
- What will the hero accomplish when he/she triumphs or dies?
- What new understanding does the hero now

have after the dust settles on the battle?

- Is this a series? Will you have a cliffhanger to lead readers to your next novel?

## 4PSS Example

I've received great feedback that this section alone, seeing the 4PSS mapped over a familiar movie/story finally turned on lightbulbs about just how 4PSS works in practice.

*Harry Potter and the Sorcerer's Stone* - J.K. Rowling

## PART 1 - Scene, Setting, Stakes
Opening scenes

- Dumbledore meets Professor McGonagall and Hagrid outside the Dursley home at night.
- Dumbledore tells McGonagall that Voldemort has killed Mr. and Mrs. Potter and tried unsuccessfully to kill their baby son, Harry.
- Dumbledore leaves Harry with an explanatory note in a basket in front of the Dursley home.
- The Dursley son, Dudley, torments and bullies Harry.
- Harry is forced to sleep in a cupboard under the stairs.

Hook

- At the zoo on Dudley's birthday, the glass in front of a boa constrictor exhibit disappears and Harry talks to it. He has special powers and can talk to snakes?

Lead up to Inciting Incident

- Harry's family flees to a lighthouse and Hagrid finds them and delivers an admissions letter to the Hogwarts School of Witchcraft and Wizardry.
- Hagrid takes Harry to shop for school supplies.
- Harry learns that his parents have left him a lot of money.
- Harry is fitted for his school uniform.
- Harry buys supplies and a magic wand—the companion wand to the evil Voldemort's.

Inciting Incident - (point of no return)

- Harry goes to the train station and catches his train to Hogwarts.

## PART 2 - Retreat, Regroup, Run

Reaction to First Plot Point - Inciting Incident

- On the train, Harry befriends other first-year students like Ron Weasley and Hermione Granger.
- Harry fears being assigned to the sinister Slytherin house by the sorting hat.
- Harry discovers that Snape does not like him.
- Professor McGonagall recommends that

Harry play Quidditch.

- Malfoy challenges Harry to a duel and Harry almost gets in trouble.

First Pinch Point - hint at evil force

- Harry accidentally discovers a fierce three-headed dog guarding a trapdoor in the forbidden third-floor corridor.

Lead up to Midpoint

- A troll is found in the building. Harry and friends defeat the troll.
- Harry's broom jerks out of control at Quidditch match.
- Harry makes a spectacular play to win the Quidditch match.

Figure out what you are up against - Midpoint

- Harry discovers the Mirror of Erised.
- Harry looks in it and sees his parents alive.
- Harry, Ron, and Hermione learn that the dog is guarding the Sorcerer's Stone.

PART 3 - Doomed Attempt to Take Action

Reaction to Midpoint

- Hagrid wins a dragon egg, but it is illegal to own dragons.
- Harry, Ron, and Hermione arrange to get rid of the dragon but get caught.
- They are all punished, and Gryffindor is docked 150 points.

Second Pinch Point - allude to evil force again

- Part of their punishment is to go into the

enchanted forest to find out who has been killing unicorns.

- In the forest, Harry comes upon a hooded man drinking unicorn blood.
- The man tries to attack Harry, but Harry is rescued by a centaur who tells him that it was Voldemort.
- Harry learns that Voldemort has been trying to steal the Sorcerer's Stone.

Reaction to Second Pinch Point

- Harry decides that he must find the stone before Voldemort does. He, Ron, and Hermione sneak to the forbidden third-floor corridor.
- They get past the guard dog and perform many impressive feats as they get closer and closer to the stone.

Lead up to Second Plot Point

- Harry ultimately finds himself face to face with Quirrell, who announces that Harry must die. Knowing that Harry wants to find the stone, Quirrell puts Harry in front of the Mirror of Erised and makes him state what he sees.
- Harry sees himself with the stone in his pocket, and at that same moment he actually feels it in his pocket. But he tells Quirrell that he sees something else.

Second Plot Point - world changed again

- A voice tells Quirrell that Harry is lying.
- Quirrell removes his turban and reveals Voldemort's face on the back of his head— Voldemort is inhabiting Quirrell's body.

## PART 4 - Climax

Accepts Reality of Situation

- Voldemort tells Quirrell to kill Harry, but Quirrell is burned by contact with the boy.

Climax Battle Scene

- A struggle ensues and Harry passes out.

New Equilibrium

- Harry wakes up in the hospital with Dumbledore.
- Dumbledore explains that he saved Harry from Quirrell. (Which in the purest form of hero 4PSS is a big no-no, because the hero has to save him or herself. Dues ex machina be damned! And that should tell you that the rules exist to be broken . . . wisely. To be fair Harry Potter is a series and at that early point in the series it's okay for the hero to get saved.)
- Harry heads down to the end-of-year banquet, where Slytherin is celebrating its win of the house championship cup.
- Dumbledore awards last-minute points to Gryffindor for Harry and friends' actions.
- Harry returns to London to spend the summer with the Dursleys.

Game, set, and match, and it doesn't get any cleaner than that story structure!

**Day 1 - Concept and Outline**

Let's go ahead and create our own little story, to see how the 4PSS simplifies the process.

I'm doing this fast and dirty as I like to, so the storyline may seem ludicrous to you as we go. However—and this is a big however—I've seen this exact type of story plot done over and over again in movies, TV, and fiction writing.

Remember, storytelling is not real life, it's entertainment. And sometimes entertainment is just so unbelievable that you say "no way," and then that very thing happens on the nightly news.

So, here we go.

**Idea—Hmmm. . . Let's call it *Death and Taxes***
Middle-aged hero guy—wife, two daughters, house, good gas mileage car, etc.—goes from downtrodden accounting guy to man on a mission to save his marriage, daughter, wife, and life from his wife's ex, a hot marine mammal laser shark researcher from Borneo. (I've seen worse plots.)

## Days 2 and 3 - Part 1: Hook to First Plot Point

Hero gets in a car accident on his two-hour commute home. He realizes that he could have been killed but that his comfortable, boring life is already doing that job slowly. When he gets home, he's ready to have hot sex with his wife and start a new life of adventure.

Unfortunately Wifey is completely through with boring husband.

Rebuff, but Wifey seems distracted by something else— Wifey's ex from high school is freshly home, visiting their small town from Borneo, where, as I said, he's a marine mammal laser shark researcher who surfs in his spare time.

## Days 4 and 5 - Part 2: First Plot Point to Midpoint

Hero tries to bring flowers, be nice, and reconnect with Wifey. Nothing works. No idea what will work, he confides in Single Drinking Buddy who tempts him with bars and meaningless sex with willing barflies.

After seeing how his bar buddy is really lonely and lost, hero knows that's where he's headed if he gives in to temptation. He vows to fight back to win back his wife's affection and, though he doesn't know it, stop her from daydreaming about marine mammal ex-guy.

## Days 6 and 7 - Part 3: Midpoint to Second Plot Point

Hero makes plan to woo wife with romance. Meanwhile, twentysomething daughter of hero bumps into steamy marine mammal ex-guy at the diner, while Wifey pines away for exciting past with her ex.

Hero's daughter invites marine mammal ex-guy to dinner where they announce that they are going to fly back to Borneo together. Wifey reveals that daughter is actually she and ex-guy's love child from 20 years ago.

The rest I don't want to spoil. We'll uncover it as we go. This is the story we'll focus on throughout the book as our example.

Get ready for "romance."

Okay, as trite and common as it may be, it only took me five minutes to write. But this story has been done a million times, so we're doing it too!

## Tips, Tools and Time

I have to admit, I love name generators. Character name generators, domain name generators, fantasy name generators. . . I even found one website that had a name generator for axes and swords.

I actually had a real need for axe names and used that site to jog my creativity enough to name the angel axes in

*The Fallen* series.

**Name generators have their place.**

When you're dead stuck, try these out. They're actually quite good. My rule on this kind of "cheat" is to use what works.

If it works, it works. If it doesn't, try something else, but don't let anyone tell you that you shouldn't. This is fiction, there is no "shouldn't."

Fun times with name and plot generators:
http://www.seventhsanctum.com/
http://www.plot-generator.org.uk/
http://writingexercises.co.uk/plotgenerator.php
http://writers-den.pantomimepony.co.uk/writers-plot-ideas.php

Your best tool is still your own imagination and asking yourself, "What if?"

And don't be afraid of anything you think, because the really good stuff will make you say to yourself, "Oh, I *really* shouldn't write that. It's too controversial and will make people angry." And that, my friend, is the exact stuff you *should* write.

I got called out by Lise on this one recently, as I got a

couple of bad Amazon reviews by people who were offended by my characters' use of profanity in *The Fallen* series.

In my mind, when I wrote them, I figured avenging archangels and demons would probably curse . . . a lot. To my surprise, not everyone shared my viewpoint.

## Committing the TIME

In a complete day, absent work and distractions, I'm asking you to commit at least 300 of the "free" minutes you have available to sharpening your writing sword—polishing your skills.

Even 120 minutes will vastly improve your skills as a writer, and make your novel speed onto the page. And I absolutely know you have 120 minutes to write each day.

Where will you get that time?

In each chapter, I'll give you a suggestion—a TTOTD, or Time Tip Of The Day.

Day 1's TTOTD comes straight from the master himself, Stephen King: "TV—while working out or anywhere else —really is about the last thing an aspiring writer needs."

Damn, now I'm quoting Stephen King, too. But he's right.

*"Kill your TV. It's busy trying to kill your creativity."* - Steve Windsor

## :: Action Steps for Day 1

- Brainstorm your high concept idea for your novel.
- Come up with two alternatives. Your main concept will evolve as you go.
- Outline your novel by filling in the Four Part Story Structure questionnaire above.
- Write one sentence for each section.
- Our word goal for "Day" 2 is 5,000-10,000.
- So block out the time—find two hours in your day. If you can, three or four hours would be better. But let's just start with getting in the habit of setting aside time to write.

## 10K A DAY Strategy

Want to become an author? Quit your day job and be your own boss? Can't quite find the time to start and finish that very first novel?

Here's the first idea to get in your nine 10,000 word days to write that precious first draft of your very first novel . . . fast.

## The "Vacation Villain"

The average—North American—vacation is about, you guessed it, nine days long. It starts Friday afternoon after work and goes to the next Sunday evening. Just about perfect for us.

Nine days . . . of "free" writing time.

Here's a tip: One time—just to get your first novel under your belt—send your family on vacation without you, and write from dawn to dusk until that first one is done. Then tell them all how awesome it is to be a real author with a real book when they get back.

This is not family abandonment, as some might suggest. This is you giving your family your very best effort to be the best writer you can be.

## Get Real Time Management!
Some have said I can be a masochist when it comes to writing in big blocks, so here's a section with more attainable time goals and suggestions on how to achieve them.

Here's the first one:

## 5K A Day Strategy

Let's call this the "technically a novel" 50,000-word strategy. Meaning, you need five hours a day. This is *totally* achievable.

If you're an early riser, try a week of setting your alarm for 5:00 AM and writing until you have to leave for work. Let's call that 7:30 AM.

Instead of waking up and having an hour's worth of prep before you can get in your car and go to work, take your shower at night, get your clothes laid out, and make a takeout breakfast ready for you to eat on your commute when you leave in the morning.

That gets you 2.5 of your hours in the morning.

Skip TV at night for a week and there's the other half of your five hours. Finding time doesn't have to be complicated.

# DAY 2: SETTING THE HOOK

**WISK**

If I were a sea captain in Neverland. . .

*"What's that? That's my hook. Looks sharp. It is."* - Steve Windsor

**What You'll Learn**

Day 2 - Part 1: The Hook

- In this section you'll learn why it's important to establish the scene, setting, and what's at stake in your hero's normal, everyday world. And you'll learn about capturing your reader's attention with a killer hook and where to put it.

Day 2 Goals:

- Write your story's hook.
- Establish the scene and settings for your novel.
- Introduce hero and establish his/her stakes.
- Write 5,000-10,000 words.

**Been There, Done That**

Scene and setting

I liked Seattle as the backdrop for *The Fallen* series. It's gray, dreary, and cold and wet almost all the time. The very place angels from Heaven or Hell would not want to go to save . . . anyone.

The futuristic setting in *The Fallen* series is marred by authoritarian rule, oppressive government, and brutal police and clergymen. It's the perfect place for the story I want to tell, which is one of treachery and revenge and oppression by not only mortal rulers but immortal gods as well.

This is why setting and scene are so important. They need to support your story—go along with the theme. If you want your reader to feel depressed, put them in a dripping prison with your hero. If you want them happy, send everyone to Hawaii on the beach or Australia or somewhere similar.

Once everyone knows where they are, or even before that, you can reveal the actual location as you deliver your compelling hook. . . Your hook needs to grab a reader by the eyeballs and not let them put down the book until they at least have to know what happens next.

In *JUMP*, I opened the book with my hero running from the authorities up a skyscraper's staircase to the roof. On the way, he's shooting at government agents and the agents are trying to kill him, all while they're all headed to the roof. This was, coincidentally, where my inciting incident decision that my hero had to make would happen— jump from the roof and die or be captured and tortured to death.

By the end of Part 1, your hero has to be faced with something that they have to deal with—they have to choose—and the reader has to care what will happen to them when they do.

## Nail on the Head

There are plenty of books about how to write scenes, character introductions, create a look and feel with your settings, and drive your reader toward the hero's inciting incident—the First Plot Point. That isn't the purpose of this book.

## Fill in the Blanks

I want you to get razor-focused on the fact that in order to get your hero to those places, you're going to fill in the blanks of certain milestones that exist in the Four Part Story Structure, based on the outline you created earlier.

By having an outline, you stop yourself from going sideways in your story and wasting time trying to recover. I want you to create a world, make something compelling happen early on, introduce your hero, and then drive him/her to a difficult decision—get him/her to the First Plot Point.

That's your job in Part 1 of your story.

To do it, you're going to block off time to write, fill in each section with enough words to satisfy the size novel you want to create—short story, novella, or novel—and then end with an "Oh my God, I can't believe that the hero has to do that!" moment.

## A Killer Hook

A great hook grabs your reader, should be inherent to the plot, and doesn't have to have action, but it should set it up. Don't waste time getting to your hook. Roll it out fast.

Hooks can serve to introduce scene, setting, stakes and even your hero. Your hook is the first chance to grab your readers by the . . . eyeballs. Make it count.

## Some Great Hooks

Sometimes opening lines can be the best hooks of all.
"In a hole in the ground there lived a hobbit."—*The Hobbit*, J.R.R. Tolkien

"In my younger and more vulnerable years my father gave

me some advice that I've been turning over in my mind ever since."—*The Great Gatsby*, F. Scott Fitzgerald

"He was an old man who fished alone in a skiff in the Gulf Stream and he had gone eighty-four days now without taking a fish."—*The Old Man and the Sea*, Ernest Hemingway

Here's my opening line from *JUMP*:
"Life's life was for eternity. That was just too damn long. My new name is Jump. This is my testament."

In *FAITH* I used a Bible quote:
"Do not suppose that I have come to bring peace to the earth. I did not come to bring peace, but a sword." (Matthew 10:34)

Cliche? Yes, however, I wanted to open by pointing out that the *Bible* is not all happiness and Heaven. That the God in the *Bible* is actually pretty vengeful. And the entire *Fallen* series depends on the reader realizing that most of what my mean, nasty angel characters say, comes directly out of the *Bible*.

Watch a movie and pay particular attention to the first five minutes. If someone doesn't get killed, run over by a car, snatched up by a demon, dumped by a boyfriend. . .

Those are all hooks. Some random wild act that doesn't

make sense yet, but will as the context of the story unfolds.

In short, the hook should suck you in so you have to find out what it meant. If you do that, you've succeeded in the only job the hook has—grab your readers by the eyeballs and keep them reading.

## Establish Setting, Scene, Stakes of Hero

Right after or during the hook, you need to establish the setting, scene, and stakes for the hero's success or failure. Where are we physically, in time, and maybe even dimension? What is the hero's normal everyday life like, and what does he/she stand to lose or win?

## Great Opening Scenes and Settings

A great setting opens us up to a new world. The best settings are in a state of change themselves. A world that is colliding with another. The setting becomes part of the plot.

A setting has its own sense of morals and justice. A prison is a great example of a setting with its own rules, code of conduct, and justice that is totally different from the outside world around it. Which leads us to the last thing.

A setting should introduce us to something that's unfamiliar, but intriguing to the reader. Suburbia to a suburbanite reader isn't all that exciting, but the wet and salty inside of a SEAL Team 6 inflatable attack raft, cutting its way through the ocean spray like a straight razor, ready to rain hate and hell down on a spy trawler disguised as a fishing boat . . . is!

Setting, scene, and stakes make your reader feel like they are inside your story.

**Our Own Little Story. . .**

Happyville is boring. It's always been boring. From the day our hero graduated high school, he and his sweetheart were destined to be . . . boring. Marriage, kids, job, car, house, death. That's how Happyville lives.

Our accountant hero guy is on another mind-numbing two-hour commute home from work, daydreaming about the coffee stains on his light blue shirt and khaki pants, when—*BAM!*—a truck smashes into him and his commuter car goes flipping down the freeway—*CRASH!* (the hook)

**Tips, Tools and Time**

Here's an article on developing a killer hook:

http://www.fictionfactor.com/guests/hookyourreader.html

Here are the top five traumas in everyday life as defined by the amount of stress they cause.

I like to have my own take on things and spice it up, so I'll call them the deadly "D's":

- Death of a loved one
- Divorce
- Displacement—moving
- Disease—major illness
- Debt—job loss

Make your hero face something like that really quickly and you'll hook most readers.

## TTOTD

Writing fiction novels is an immersive act. What I mean by that is that in order to take your reader into a world in their mind, you must first immerse yourself in that world. You have to rip yourself away from the distractions and doldrums of everyday life.

Get your head out of your cell phone, off your email, and away from your social media suck, and enter the world of wonder inside your story. That takes more than five minutes.

**You need big blocks of time.** Here's a story about why.

Shortly after college, I worked on a home construction

crew. (Who knew all that expensive education would qualify me for that job, right?) One thing I vividly remember from that experience was the time it took to set up and tear down production each day.

In the morning, we pulled out tools, dragged extension cords, unloaded lumber, drank a little coffee, cleared the night's water and debris from the work area (being Seattle, there was always water). . . It was a good solid 30 minutes before our construction crew was up and running, ready to pound one single nail. In general, we only *prepared* to work.

Since boards and nails are the things that build houses and in return make money, all of that prep work in the morning and the reverse of it in the evening made no money at all. That's no different from writing.

You won't hit your stride and start "nailing" words until you are sucked into your world. And that, my friend, is not a five-minute process.

Schedule in blocks of uninterrupted time so you can get into your world. Make it known that you're not to be disturbed during that time, and then don't allow yourself to be.

It's more efficient and will actually cause you to have to work less on your novel than if you work in shorter blocks of time, more often.

## :: Action Steps for Day 2

- Figure out what your hero wants.
- Write your killer hook.
- Use it to establish scene, setting, and stakes for the hero.
- Force your hero toward the inciting incident.
- Our word goal for "Day" 3 is 5,000-10,000.
- So block out the time: 5-10 hours.

You can do this over the course of days if you have to, but try to get blocks of at least two hours set aside.

## 10K A DAY Strategy

Been to Disneyland? How many times? How many times do you think they change everything about it? Not very often.

Remember that last 10K A DAY tip? "Vacation Villain?" Well, this one is a variation of it.

Behold **"Disneyland Destruction"**

Any way you want. The next trip to a theme park, thrill ride, carnival, or other "attraction" time waster, send your spouse with the kids—forgo it all together—or simply go and hole up in the hotel the entire time . . . writing.

Hey, you'll be there for dinner and breakfast and you can take a break to watch the fireworks on Saturday night, but they will *all* be there next year . . . and so will your novel. Because it will be written and published.

Family abandonment? You're showing your commitment to your writing!

## 5K A DAY Strategy

Okay, I'm warming up to the kinder, gentler novel-writing strategy.

I actually have a novella that I have to write and offer as a prologue, freebie, enticer for *The Fallen* series. It's called *STEG*. Writing 50,000 in a week is like a breather week for me, so here's another technique you can use to get your five hours.

7:00 PM to 12:00 AM can get you some quality back-to-back hours. Five hours is a good immersion block.

Don't think I don't know that five hours can leave you wiped out. I've done it many times. So when I'm writing at home, if I hit a pause point and need a quick break, I stand up and do jumping jacks or some push-ups. Once the blood is flowing again, I'm back at it.

# DAY 3: IMPOSSIBLE DECISIONS

## WISK

*"What is that thing? That's my foreshadow, baby."* - Steve Windsor

## What You'll Learn

Day 3 - Part 1: Lead Up and First Plot Point

- In this section we'll talk about foreshadowing, setting up the inciting incident, and driving your hero toward the First Plot Point.
- Why it's important to herd him or her towards an inevitable decision that will change his or her world irrevocably into the future.

## Been There, Done That

In *The Fallen* series, I slather on foreshadowing to the point of drowning my readers.

As *The Fallen* is a 10-book series/saga, I'm free to have my characters say or do things in their book/episode that may or may not be resolved by the end of that particular novel (another advantage of a series). However, I reveal meanings in later books where I absolutely want someone to have to go back to an earlier book and find that place.

Then they see that I almost hit them over the head that it would happen.

The angels in this series are all-knowing beings who experience time differently than Man does, and as such, they know events to come, those in the past, and what will happen in the present. They are free to spout sarcastic comments like, "Don't want to lose your head twice in one eternity, now do you?" And whomever they are talking to will be completely confused by the statement, because they have never lost their head. But you can bet they'll literally lose their head exactly twice by the end of the series.

**Nail on the Head**

An excellent use of foreshadowing is the movie *Jaws*. In Part 2, when the grizzled shark hunter, Quint, describes his ordeal during WWII of his ship blowing up and all his shipmates being adrift in the ocean for days, we're riveted.

When Quint tells of the screams of those men as sharks came and picked them off one by one, we're terrified at the thought. This sets up the almost inevitable "boat sinks and Quint gets eaten by shark" scene between Parts 3 and 4 of *Jaws*.

**Set up the Inciting Incident**

If the inciting incident is supposed to change the hero's life forever, we'd better have a pretty good idea of why. The only way to do that is to show enough of the hero's life before the inciting event happens. That way we know why the event upsets the hero's nice little world.

In addition to leading up to the inciting incident, you must accomplish a number of other things in Part 1. We already talked about setting and scene, but you must also make it clear what type of story you're telling—mystery, thriller, adventure, love story.

Finally, Part 1 should introduce most, if not all, of the characters who will play a significant part in the story's plot.

Foreshadowing. . . Two words—**Lone Star**. You'll see why later.

## Foreshadow Coming Events

Part 1 of any story is mainly setup for the future misery and mayhem or mourning that will befall the hero in Part 2. As you drive the hero through Part 1, toward the inciting incident, foreshadowing becomes a tool to hint at other elements that will arrive later in your story.

For a somewhat humorous example, if you show your

hero cooking sizzling bacon in Part 1, somewhere in Parts 2, 3, or 4 our hero may have to fight his way through a pig stampede.

If you've ever heard a character in the early stages of a movie say, "That never happens," somewhere before the end of the story, whatever "that" was, will most surely happen.

And that warrants a quick note about unneeded story elements. There's an old adage that if you show a knife on a table in Part 1, someone better get stabbed by that knife by the end of the story, otherwise it was needless to show it.

A generous use of foreshadowing in Part 1 can set subliminal expectations in the reader of things to come. Done well, it keeps a reader engaged and wondering, "What did that mean?" And when its meaning is revealed, in the back of their mind, the reader should think, "Ah-ha!"

## Set up Your Hero's Impossible Decision

That's what the inciting incident will be. You must give your hero a decision they have to make, but make it unavoidably painful either way. Take Katniss Everdeen in *The Hunger Games*.

Once you know where Katniss is, that her sister and

mother are reliant on her, that they live in squalor, her dad is dead, and her world is gone to an authoritarian hell. You see that she's figured out how to make do by hunting to stave off the starvation that most people are subjected to. She does that by defying the law and authorities. We know she's a rebellious type.

To drive Part 1 to the inciting incident, you have to lead your hero closer and closer to a decision that he or she will have to make at the end of Part 1.

In *The Hunger Games*, Katniss and her boyfriend go hunting in the woods. An illegal act, we are told. When the Capitol's shuttle appears and they both discuss the Reaping to come, this is how we know that something bad is coming. The reminder literally flies right over their heads.

By the time the townspeople get to the center of the city and the tributes are announced, it is clear that the Hunger Games are a death sentence.

## Inciting Incident—the First Plot Point

When Katniss' sister, Primrose, is selected in the Reaping to be in the Hunger Games, it's a death sentence for her younger sibling. Two things have been set up for us.

Number one, we care. Who wouldn't care about a girl trying to feed and care for her impoverished and oppressed family?

Number two, we know Katniss is a good person with a horrible decision to make—volunteer as tribute and probably be killed, or let her sister be taken to her certain death. Now that's an exciting Inciting Incident!

**Our Own Little Story. . .**

His little commute car crash lands hero guy in the hospital, where he has a revelation—he's going to die a boring, meaningless old man in a loveless marriage.

Meanwhile, Wifey doesn't even show at the hospital because she's home pining away with her mobile phone on mute, looking at old high school pictures of her with her ex-boyfriend. She knows he's coming back to town from Borneo soon, where he lives as a marine mammal biologist researching laser sharks, while surfing for fun from his grass hut house on the beach. (I hate those high school exes.)

Hero husband is released from the hospital and has to call his single drinking buddy to come pick him up and take him home. When hero gets home, Wifey is concerned, but distracted.

Husband realizes Wifey has been acting strangely lately. Going to the salon, worrying about her weight, giving him the cold shoulder, and that evil eye at dinner? And though he was just almost killed, she seems less than concerned or interested in his health.

Now, before hero has time to ponder Wifey's strange behavior and put anything together in his mind, Wifey announces that she wants a divorce! (inciting incident) And as a side dish, Wifey wants to keep custody of their minor daughter and have their 20-year-old daughter stay with her too.

Hero guy has to move out of house, she says!

**Tips, Tools and Time**

Be subtle about foreshadowing. It doesn't have to knock the reader over the head. Just sprinkle it.

**Keep track of your foreshadowing.**

I have a huge spreadsheet of character vocabulary, vices, and other useful information I can reference about plots and notes. One of the sheets is labeled "Things to reconcile." I reference that sheet to make sure that I tie up loose ends that I created earlier.

You can do this inside Scrivener—it has a pretty rich character template. However, I find it easier to scroll through characters in a spreadsheet.

So, if on page 50 I say that my character somehow knows how to cure a disease, I clean it up in another place by showing him actually doing it.

## Inciting Incident
In short, the inciting incident means impossible decisions to make, usually between bad and worse. Setting your hero on his or her quest for understanding.

## TTOTD

Did you know that there's no law that says you have to eat, take a shower, get dressed, go outside, or even get out of bed unless you have to go to work?

Even then [cough, cough], I think I have the H1N1DL virus today [Hack hack]. H1N1DL? Have 1 Novel 1 Day Left to write it.

"Mental health day." Say it with me. (Of course, I say this tongue-in-cheek as you would never really do that . . . would you?)

But there *are* mornings on the weekend when I simply reach next to my bed, grab my laptop, open it to where I left off . . . and start writing again.

## :: Action Steps for Day 3

- Detail events leading your hero toward the inciting incident.
- Judiciously apply foreshadowing of things to come later as you do.
- Write a killer inciting incident—irrevocable and unavoidable decision that your hero has to make.
- Literally force your hero to choose between bad and worse.
- Our word goal for "Day" 4 is 5,000-10,000.
- So block out the time: 5-10 hours.

## 10K A DAY Strategy

Here's a "by now you know there will be discomfort" way to find the time to get your novel written.

## The **"Month of Misery"**

A month happens to have four weekends . . . usually. Some are better and we get five. But let's keep it simple. Four weekends—eight days to write.

But Steve, where are we going to get that ninth day? I'm glad you asked. Because one of the Fridays or Mondays before or after one of those weekends, one of your distant . . . distant relatives is going to . . . "die." [Dr. Evil touches pinky to corner of mouth again.]

Seriously, I'm sorry for your loss, but you're going to have to tell work that your fifth cousin's grandma's cat died and you have to go to the funeral.

I nicknamed this one the "Four Weekends and a Funeral" strategy for writing your next novel.

I hope you realize by now that I say all of this as a way to spur you to prioritize your writing dream. I literally write this way and then take weeks off between written words. I'm merely trying to introduce you to an alternative to the "write a little every day" advice that is doled out so ubiquitously.

You can write this way. Is there sacrifice? Every decision sacrifices something else.

**5K A DAY Strategy**

I used to take the BART (Bay Area Rapid Transit) into San Francisco to work every day. The ride was about 45 minutes each way, sitting down. I've written on public transit with my laptop and I've even done it on my mobile phone.

You can get in 1.5 hours on your commute. Don't do it while you're driving—not recommended.

Then if you get a lunch break at work, instead of going to lunch with colleagues, go to a coffeehouse and write for an hour. One hour.

If they've taken your one hour lunch away too, use the thirty minutes that you hopefully have left to write your way toward getting out from under their oppressive management.

Boring meeting that someone *had* to schedule at work? You can sneak in 30-60 minutes in one of those.

No? Yes, I've done it.

You know those meetings are counterproductive anyway. Might as well get some writing time.

That just leaves you with two hours to knock out after work. No TV show and you're done.

# DAY 4: RUN FOR YOUR LIFE!

## WISK

*"Why are you running? Because everyone else is walking."* - Steve Windsor

## What You'll Learn

Day 4 - Part 2: Reaction to the First Plot Point

- You'll learn how to transition from the First Plot Point. What will your hero do now that they have made their impossible decision?
- You'll learn why it's important for your hero to flail and fail in the early stages of Part 2. This section is aptly nicknamed, "Run for your life."
- And you'll learn that anything our hero tries to do in this section, knee-jerk reaction or half-hearted attempt . . . will fail miserably and only get him or her into worse trouble.

## Been There, Done That

Part 2 in the 4PSS is arguably one of the hardest sections to write. It's more difficult as you approach the midpoint of your novel, but for your hero, Part 2 is a no-man's-land of wandering and wondering what the hell's going on.

At some point in Part 2, you'll question if you know what you're trying to accomplish with your story.

Follow your 4PSS outline. Part 2 is why you made it.

## Spoiler Alert

In *JUMP*, once I established that my hero had to choose Heaven or Hell, and once he slightly, unwittingly but not really, chose, I sent him into a birth cycle of becoming a being that he had no idea how to be.

He sprouted wings he didn't know how to use, hallucinated in dreams that were terrible and that he couldn't separate from reality, and in general, just literally flew around getting his ass kicked and his guts pecked out. In short, he was lost and running for his life.

## Nail on the Head

In the beginning of Part 2, your hero has to be lost and bewildered with no idea what just happened (inciting incident) or what to do about it. They're whisked into a world or life or situation that they don't understand or maybe even knew existed.

## Some examples would be:
An accountant being sent to a brutal prison - *The Shaw-*

Katniss thrown on the train and rocketing towards the capitol - *The Hunger Games*

Harry after the train to Hogwarts. He arrives in a world he knows nothing about. - *Harry Potter and the Sorcerer's Stone.*

## Reaction to First Plot Point

Your hero's reaction to the First Plot Point, when his/her world is turned upside down, has to be one of at least initial bewilderment.

The First Plot Point's job is to introduce unwanted conflict. The hero's reaction to that conflict can't be too self-assured or even effective. In short, your hero is now lost. He/she has to retreat, regroup, run.

If your hero is too powerful or skilled or knowledgeable right after the FPP, there's nothing for him or her to overcome. No triumph over "self" in trying times.

The reader has to empathize with the hero's plight and be able to root for him or her as the hero grows.

## Retreat, Regroup, Run

This is exactly what we want a hero to do at the beginning of Part 2—run for their very lives! There's no understanding, there's nothing they can do to make it better, and they just want to escape.

The hero can't, of course, but you have to make them run around crazy and try.

No one will believe your hero, no one will help them, and no one's coming to save them.

"Fire, hot! I gotta get out of this house!"

Not, find a fire extinguisher, spray it down, save the day, and then call the fire department to come clean up. Then there's no story left to tell.

Make your hero run!

## Doomed Attempt to Take Action

Any action the hero *does* take in Part 2 is so doomed to catastrophic failure that it wouldn't even be worth rooting for them.

If he/she even offers resistance to a bully, that bully will pound them resoundingly in Part 2. We'll leave the "almost" fight back for Part 3.

In fact, if your inciting incident is a bully at a new school beating up your hero, then in Part 2 the entire school is going to laugh at them. And if your hero tells the principal, he or she will somehow end up getting into trouble for it.

## Our Own Little Story. . .

Our hero guy begs Wifey to reconsider the divorce. She's adamant—get out! Hero runs to single drinking buddy's house for consoling. He ends up drinking at a bar with single buddy.

After too many drinks, drinking buddy convinces hero guy that wife is a mean person and he's better off.

Hero guy drives them home in drinking buddy's car, wrecks, gets arrested for driving while intoxicated, and thrown in jail for the night.

Everything your hero does, makes things worse.

## Tips, Tools and Time

The middle of your novel is about death. Yes, death. It's the moment before and the moment after something in your hero dies . . . right in front of you and your audience.

Everything before that, he thought or felt a certain way; everything after, he or she will never be the same again.

There are three types of death: physical, professional, and psychological. And it's at this midpoint moment that your novel reveals what it's all about. And that's where we're headed in the next chapter—death.

## TTOTD

Learn to skim-read. There are simply so many books out there on how to do . . . anything, really. But, how-to books on writing are everywhere. Some are good, some are not so good, but all have something in them that will help you.

Skim how-to books to find the meat. You'll see it, trust me. That's what I did when I got stuck on this middle section. I told you it was hard to write the middle. And that's when I came across and skimmed the book that gave me the "idea" for the death analogy above.

Credit where credit is due, I'll give you a link to that helpful novel-writing book in the next chapter, because I had no idea what I was up against in writing this book.

So now . . . I have to figure out what I'm up against. So do you. And so does your hero.

### :: Action Steps for Day 4
- Write your hero's reaction to First Plot Point scenes.

- A few thousand words on your hero running around like a chicken with his/her head cut off, yelling the sky is falling (plot point one—inciting incident) and only getting ridicule in return. Because the sky may very well indeed be falling, but there's nothing your hero can do about it . . . until tomorrow.
- Give your hero something to do, try, or trip over, but make sure he/she falls flat on their face.
- Our word goal for "Day" 5 is 5,000-10,000.

## 10K A DAY Strategy

The **"Weekend Warrior"**

Sounds kinda cool, huh? Here's the schedule:

You have a life, you have to punch the clock at work. You want to be an author, but you have to pay the bills. Guess what, they still have to give you weekends off . . . mostly.

So here's the specific schedule that you can use on that "Four Weekends and a Funeral" idea I gave you last time. It's not easy—I never promised that, did I?

1 - Plow your way home through the traffic of your miserable commute. (Two hours max, otherwise you need to consider moving.)

2 - 7:00 PM - 12:00 AM You're gonna write, baby! Grab pizza, take-out Chinese, I don't care—we're writing!

3 - Set your alarm and get up at 6:00 AM - Beg spouse, roommate, or dog to go get you some coffee and a slice of toast and . . . start writing in bed.

The added benefit to this one is I'm not even going to make you get out of bed today . . . all day long! Who wouldn't love that day.

And guess where I am as I type this very line. In bed, with the coffee my wife brought for me (thank you, dear), and she and my daughters left for the day to go to their cousins' house all day.

Family abandonment? There are many other jobs—airline pilot friends of mine for example, where they fly around the world for two weeks and then are off for two weeks. That's what I'm advocating here—intense focus, then relax and take some days away from it, and then rinse and repeat.

4 - 12:01 PM Get out of bed and relieve yourself and get something to munch on and then get back into bed. I know, this is awesome!

5 - 12:15 PM to 6:00 PM Write! How simple is that? **Make**

**sure you turned that damn cell phone off** . . . or at least on vibrate if you're a "Dr." and simply *must* be on call. Otherwise, the world doesn't need you to keep itself spinning.

6 - 6:00 PM to 6:15 PM Another break? Wow!

7 - 6:15 PM Scrape lunch and breakfast crumbs out of bed . . . and then get back to writing.

8 - 12:00 AM Wake up! Stop sleeping on the job! Okay, you're finished for the day. Set your alarm for 6:00 AM again.

Tomorrow—Sunday—**rinse and repeat.**

Total time—29 hours, baby! BAM! One-third of your novel is written. At this pace, it will only take you three week-ends to finish.

If one of your resolutions was to write a novel this year. Wahoo! Take the rest of the year off!

## 5K A DAY Strategy

If you're a stay-at-home mom or dad, I can empathize. My daughters keep me busy.

I used to give my wife hell when I was commuting and

she was at home with our kids. I teased her that all she did was go to Starbucks all day. Uh, wrong!

However, I can write an absolute ton while my daughters are in school. Instead of going home and fretting over how the house looks and wasting time trying to make it look better when I know it's just getting trashed again after school, I go to a coffeehouse and write.

Man, I'm a hypocrite. I can't believe it. Shh, don't tell my wife.

# DAY 5: FIGURING THINGS OUT

**WISK**

*"Oh, you're an evil little flirt, aren't you. Just figured that out, huh?"* - Steve Windsor

**What You'll Learn**

Day 5 - Part 2: First Pinch Point to Midpoint

In this section, the second half of Part 2 of your story, you'll learn how to introduce the evil force that's behind your hero's troubles. Then we'll write your hero's reaction to that if he/she has any at all, and then you'll write your hero to the midpoint. There, your hero will finally figure out what he or she is up against.

As I've said, Part 2 is probably the toughest part to write. But it's also the toughest part for your hero to go through, so it's fitting that you both struggle during this section.

In Part 2, the saying goes, your characters can fumble, flail, and even fornicate with each other, but they can't free themselves from the unknown force that has been set upon them by their decision in Part 1.

Yet by the end of Part 2, your hero will come face to face

with the force that's trying to kill him or her and finally understand it.

**Been There, Done That**

When I wrote *FURY,* the second book in *The Fallen* series, I was a little more seasoned. I had learned to follow the Four Part Story Structure almost religiously. (That's a pun, because *The Fallen* is a religious thriller series and. . . Get it? . . . Oh, never mind. Sorry.)

Regardless, by then, I loved my characters so much and wanted them to succeed and win so badly, that it was difficult for me to let them fall on their faces during Part 2, much less allow them to face death.

I mean, I was right there causing their suffering and holding the key to ending it . . . literally at the tips of my fingers. But I had to let them fail and learn and explore and love and hate. Otherwise, there was no story to tell, right?

**Nail on the Head**

In Part 2 you, as an author, are like a mother or father who doesn't want your children to get hurt, but know you have to let them fend for themselves.

So when you feel yourself hating the evil villains causing

your hero's misery, and you want nothing more than to have your hero turn around and defeat them . . . don't. You are exactly where you should be.

If you've ever watched a horror movie, you can see the Part 2 scenes in bloody red detail. It's the part where you hold your hand over your eyes and say out loud, "Don't go in there, stupid!" or "He's got a knife, idiot!"

Horror movie heroes make decisions like hiding in a shed full of power tools, or tapping a hunched-over wife on the shoulder, only to find out she's turned into a zombie and is eating the family dog.

Once the "Jason" character in the hockey mask pops out of the closet (inciting incident), every trip and fall in a horror movie is Part 2 mayhem and misery.

## First Pinch Point

Midway between the inciting incident and the midpoint, a few scenes into the hero's reaction to the First Plot Point, you need to introduce your readers to the evil force facing your hero.

You may or may not choose to show it to your hero yet, but the audience needs a hint as to why all this is happening. And you're going to give it to them. Just a little sprinkle of evil. . .

## Reaction to Pinch Point

The reaction to the First Pinch Point may not even come from our hero, but something will happen in reaction to it.

Betty at the salon will tell our hero's wife that she just saw her ex get off the bus at the bus station (something our hero's wife obviously already knows is coming).

And this will cause our hero's wife to display even more random and unexplained behavior in the presence of our hero.

And you can bet, later on, when our hero does bump into the evil-force boyfriend, that guy won't have two kids, a pot belly, and a two-hour commute.

## Lead up to Midpoint

I'm kind of liking our little romance-novel segue, so let's keep going with that.

Our hero will bump and blather about, begging his "acting strangely" wife to reconsider divorce for most of the first half of Part 2.

He has no idea what's causing his wife's behavior change and no idea what to do about the fact that she wants a divorce. That's exactly where we want him—in the dark, struggling the whole time.

By the midpoint, our hero's "death," hero guy will come face to face with the realization that Wifey doesn't love him anymore and is pining away for marine mammal ex-guy.

## Midpoint of the Story

Figure out what you're up against.

Like I said, at the midpoint of our novel, our hero husband is going to have to realize that his wife's ex-boyfriend from high school is back in town. And he'll also realize that's why she's been acting strangely and wants a divorce. In short, he'll meet the evil force face to face—figure out what he's up against.

This revelation comes at the exact middle of your novel. If your novel is 50,000 words long, then at 25,000 our hero will bump into his wife's ex and the part of him that still believes he can salvage things with his wife . . . will die.

That doesn't mean he'll have any idea what to do about it. In fact, he won't, because in Part 3 he's going to react to this new understanding—midpoint revelation—and try and try to do something about it.

Right now, by the end of Part 2, we just want our hero to have a proverbial "raised eyebrow" moment. "So that's why!" he or she will say. "I had no idea."

And if you did your job correctly, made your hero flail around reacting to his wife's strange behavior and ultimatum with no hope or understanding of what to do about it or what's causing it, that'll be the exact truth. Your hero will have had no idea what he was up against before, but now he or she will. And faced with the death of his or her delusions, our hero will now have to act. (Part 3)

That's the split between Parts 2 and 3—the before and after.

**Our Own Little Story. . .**

In our love story, which as you may have already guessed I don't write much of, this may be the place where the high school boyfriend of our hero's wife shows up back in town at the bus station after being gone for over 20 years.

And your audience will go, "That's why she's been going crazy at the salon, working out, and fighting with her husband—our hero—so much!" Our hero doesn't have to see the evil force—old boyfriend—get off the bus, but the audience does.

The ex is why Wifey wanted the divorce! SOB!

## Tips, Tools and Time

I know I said that Part 2 was difficult to write, but it doesn't have to be. You can have all kinds of fun with your hero in Part 2.

Picture your hero as someone you don't necessarily hate, but that you aren't that fond of either. Maybe someone who's rude to you in line at a coffee shop, or a girlfriend who said something behind your back, or maybe a guy who said he was busy and couldn't go out Saturday, but then you bump into him at a bar with another girl.

Now, you don't hate the hero or wish them harm, so much as you have contempt for him or her. What would you want to have happen to that person now?

Not mortal injury, just . . . playful misfortune.

Maybe the girl at the bar would spill her drink on the guy who turned her down. Or maybe someone would hit and run the gossiping girlfriend's car.

In our little fictitious romance, maybe our hero husband would lose his job just as the ex-boyfriend is getting off the bus. And when he tries to garner some sympathy from his wife, she's completely unsympathetic because she's daydreaming about the ex.

But by the time you're finished with your hero in Part 2, he or she will face the death of his body, mind, or psyche.

**TTOTD**
- Write on the train on your commute.
- Let your spouse drive and write on that four-hour drive to the mountains to take the family away for the weekend.
- I have written on my notes application on my mobile phone while I was on a long hike. Then I cut and paste it into email and sent it to myself to drop into Scrivener.

I know I've emphasized big blocks of time, but I'm not above stitching together a 10-hour day out of the minutes in between "life." I've written at the DMV, waiting for my number to be called. That could easily take five hours.

**:: Action Steps for Day 5**
- Write your hero's reaction to First Pinch Point —the introduction of the evil force.
- A few thousand words on the consequences for your hero after the evil force rears its ugly head.
- Our word goal for "Day" 6 is 5,000-10,000.
- So block out the time: 5-10 hours.

In our romance, maybe the hero tries to initiate sex with his wife to make himself feel better at how crappy things are going, only to get the proverbial "headache" treatment.

Give your hero misfortune to endure, but no way to understand it until the midpoint. Then pull back the covers and, "Surprise, the ex-boyfriend's in town!"

And a really good way to do that is to have the hero walk in on the wife sorting through old photo albums that just happen to contain photos of her and the marine mammal ex.

Then at lunch, hero and a coworker, who just happens to be female, will go to lunch and—BAM!—bump right into Wifey's ex. And at that point, our hero's attractive coworker will comment afterward that marine mammal boy looks hotter than he did in high school.

Careful here, it's a fine line between revelation and plot point, so don't have the hero catch his wife and the ex in bed. That's a plot point!

## BONUS
James Scott Bell: *Write Your Novel From The Middle*

I'm not going to try and re-write Mr. Bell's book, but simply put out his idea of starting your story in the middle. It's one worth researching and is definitely a perspective that will add to your toolkit as an author.

I skimmed it, liked it, and will give more attention to the dreaded middle pages of my novels on my next write. And like I said, find the ideas and then use them or don't.

## 10K A DAY Strategy

This one's a toughie and I know I'm going to get some backlash, but good writing is about conflict, remember?

I call this one **"Cheating Jesus."**

It's actually how I wrote my third published novel, *FAITH*.

Nine of the 12 days of Christmas, I wrote. (Hey, I'm leaving you with three days, how many can Christmas possibly take?)

Until just now, deep into editing, I failed to see the irony in *how* I wrote a novel called *"FAITH"* by skipping Christmas.

The universe—you gotta love it.

## 5K A DAY Strategy

In our reduced-pain version of the *Nine Day Novel,* we need to write 45-50,000 words to complete our novel.

By now, we know there are four weekend days in that nine-day period, so we could actually hammer out 40 of those 45 hours on those weekend days, and then only have to write an hour a day during our work week.

If we didn't want to do that though, we could get up early on Saturday and Sunday—7:00 AM—and write for half days. Then take the rest of the day off—12:00 to whenever we wanted.

That gives us 20,000 words and now we only need our weekday 25 hours.

# DAY 6: FIGHT BACK, FAIL

## WISK

*"Foreshadow, huh? Yep. Well, what was that then? That was my . . . midpoint."* - Steve Windsor

## What You'll Learn

Day 6 - Part 3: Midpoint to Second Pinch Point and Reaction

In this section we'll talk about how to set your hero on a pathway to redemption. Our hero has seen "death" and now knows that he or she must fight to survive. We aren't offering redemption itself just yet, only the pathway. There's still much failure ahead.

I know, it's just horrible to endure, isn't it? Especially since we normally love our characters. But in Part 3 our hero is still doomed to failure, though he or she will make a more concerted and planned-out attempt at success in this section.

But before that, our hero has to recover from the revelation of understanding what he's up against. He has to freak out a little and still be a little bewildered at what to do about it.

At least now the threat is known, or our hero thinks it is, because at the end of Part 3, we are going to rip the rug out from under his or her hard-won understanding of what he's facing.

## Been There, Done That

Twists and turns. The road to understanding is windy, but trying to figure out what to do about it is going to be a brick wall for our hero.

In my third novel in *The Fallen* series, *FAITH*, I followed my hero in two different time periods (he has three). I followed him in the present as an old blaspheming priest who is supposedly scared of his own shadow, and I flash-back-followed him from when he was a young boy through attending the seminary.

As an older priest, he'd forgotten all the trials and much of what he endured as a young boy and was slowly remembering those lessons all over again on his journey to understanding his part in an overall plot by the Devil himself.

Where things get complicated in a series is that at the same time you're taking one novel and one hero through the Four Part Story Structure, you need to overlay that same structure and expand it out to your entire series.

Even a series has the four parts, because at some point an audience wants resolution, even if you cliffhanger them every season.

So *The Fallen* books 1-3 are Part 1 of the overall story, Books 4-6 are Part 2, books 7-8 are Part 3, and Books 9 and 10 are the Climax in Part 4.

So in this third book in the series, while my hero is figuring himself out in Part 3 of his own book, the end of his book is just about the point where everyone in the series still has to be confused about the overall evil force and barely get to the inciting incident—First Plot Point of the series.

Believe me, spreadsheets help with this, because you can outline and overlay the 4PSS of the series onto all the mini (novel) 4PSS underneath its umbrella.

I had to be careful to let my hero fight back and lose small battles in his own Part 3, and I had to do that while not revealing anything more than Part 1 Setup for the series as a whole. And then reveal a Part 1 inciting series incident at the end of Faith's book.

## Nail on the Head

Let's expand on our series explanation as it relates to our

beginning of Part 3.

*The Hunger Games* "trilogy," though as the movie franchise made clear, the story had to be broken into a classic 4PSS by splitting the third book into 2 parts—Mockingjay 1 and 2.

*The Hunger Games* - Setup (4PSS Part 1)

This is Katniss' world and what it's like. Katniss triumphs over those hunger games, but is stuck now with evil president who watches her every move and will kill her if she isn't good.

*The Hunger Games: Catching Fire* - Figure things out (4PSS Part 2)

We see that the president is so evil he wants to kill Katniss and will do anything, even break the rules of the Hunger Games, to do it.

At the end of this book, we figure out that some of the bad guys in the revolution are good guys in disguise and some people have sacrificed themselves for the greater good to save Katniss. But in the process, Katniss loses Peeta, whom she's arguably falling in love with.

Katniss is saved and now understands that there is a revolution afoot, but she has no idea what to do about it.

But she knows she must save Peeta. Classic story structure Part 2. Book 2 equals Part 2. Are you seeing this?

*The Hunger Games: Mockingjay Part 1* (4PSS Part 3)—Fight back lose

Katniss decides to join the revolution and help so that she can get Peeta back—a proactive reaction that's doomed to failure.

She fights valiantly and seemingly wins, but when she gets Peeta back—surprise!—he's a brainwashed assassin who wants to choke her to death and kill her! Classic fight back and lose story structure Part 3.

Damn that story is good!

*The Hunger Games: Mockingjay Part 2* (4PSS part 4)—Fight back win

In the end, we don't even have to see the movie to know that the president is going to be defeated, Katniss will probably get Peeta back, but she'll lose her initial love interest to do it.

Climax battle scene revolution succeeds at great cost, everyone kinda gets what they want and the lesson is learned. Authoritarian government is bad and brutal and will cost you dearly defeating it.

Wakey-wakey people!

Back to Part 3. . . So our job in Part 3 is to give our hero courage—enough fight against the evil he or she now thinks she recognizes as trying to kill him or her, literally or figuratively, all the while realizing that we aren't going to let him or her win.

Our hero has yet to learn the true nature of the evil that is against him or her. That's what we'll reveal in the Second Plot Point.

**Reaction to Midpoint**

Back to our fake romance story.

Our hero husband now knows that his wife's ex is back in town. He understands what he's up against. He's put two and two together and come up with, "Ex boyfriend is still on my wife's mind and making her act strangely and wanting a divorce. Now I have to do something about it."

And from there he can go all kinds of ways. He has enough information to now make a concerted effort to repair his marriage, leave his wife (yet even that won't be simple because they have two children. Did I mention that?) or remove the ex-boyfriend from the story, so to speak.

Whatever he chooses, the hero now has information he can use to help him make a more concerted effort at repairing his faltering life/marriage. Unfortunately . . . it ain't gonna work.

## Second Pinch Point

The Second Pinch Point's job is to remind our audience of the evil force lurking in the shadows of the subtext of our novel. There's still something unknown and fishy going on in now-not-so-Happyville. It's our job to sift it out for the reader, without spoiling the Second Plot Point.

Oh, Darth Vader, how you mock me!

In our little romance we could do this by having our hero's oldest daughter bump into mommy's newly returned ex at the diner downtown. And marine mammal ex-guy may know who she is, but she won't know who he is. And there may be some kind of tension in the exchange that has our reader saying, "Uh-oh, that is *so* not good."

What this tension signifies has to be a mystery to our reader and our hero. In fact, once again, the hero may not even know about the Second Pinch Point or. . . What if at dinner that night—because at least hero guy isn't moving out of house—while Wifey is daydreaming about marine mammal ex-guy and our hero is brooding and plotting in his mind about what to do about divorce, daughter casually mentions she ran into the "new" guy that everyone in town is talking about.

Now the dinner conversation perks up and Wifey is out of her daydream, our hero is steaming, and daughter is clueless. And something is rotten in Happyville.

The reader may have a clue as to what it is, but the hero still doesn't know for sure.

### Tips, Tools and Time

Think evil. Now think more evil. Now think unthinkable evil. That's the stuff people wanna read.

### Use temptation.

In our romance, our hero may just brood at dinner while finally understanding his wife's behavior and preoccupation. Have him go over options of what he could do about it with his drinking buddy, who just happens to be single with none of the difficulties our hero is experiencing.

In fact, a good thing to do is to tempt your hero, now that he knows about wife's ex, by throwing a willing young waif in front of him at the bar. Then have his friend encourage him to go for it. (All heroes have tempting friends like that, don't they?)

See how your hero reacts to temptation now that he fully understands what's going on in his cracked-apart world. You may be surprised what he or she does.

## TTOTD

One thing you definitely don't want to do as you write is edit. But it's an irresistible impulse to go back and read over what you just wrote. That does two things: slows you down and activates your monkey brain critic that sits on your shoulder and tells you that your writing sucks.

I'll admit, wink-wink, that I do fix obvious misspellings and double-spaces as I go. It's quick and dirty, but I try not to re-read for story and plot.

## :: Action Steps for Day 6

- Write your hero's reaction to the midpoint— understand what you're up against.
- A few thousand words about how your hero reacts to finally understanding why every-thing that he's running and ranting about is happening.
- Introduce your evil force again. This time make it more sinister and more foreboding. Make your audience fear for your hero be-cause of it.
- Our word goal for "Day" 7 is 5,000-10,000.

- So block out the time: 5-10 hours.

## 10K A DAY Strategy

Once again, this book is a little American-centric, but you can take any national holiday and apply the same tactics. So, no more Cinco de Mayo tequila for you!

## "Patriot Punishment"

Fourth of July holiday in the US is a great time to blow off some steam, get drunk, and overeat at a family picnic. It also happens to be a fantastic time to skip all that non-sense . . . and write your novel!

Depending on when it falls, the average working citizen gets four to five days off around the Fourth of July. Use them to write half your novel!

I'm not saying you have to do all of these, but surely there's one of them that you could try.

## 5K A DAY Strategy

I absolutely will not slight the difficulty it takes to carve out time while you are the main caregiver to kids. Single moms, dads too, hats off to you. But if you still want to make that change—chase after your dream of writing—something *has* to be done.

My daughters are getting to the age where they can do their homework, make their own food, and read to themselves. And when they do that, it's the perfect time to write. (Of course there'll be interruptions and you should plan for that. Sometimes this works for me and sometimes daddy stops and helps with homework or reads a story to my girls. I know I'm going to make up the time somewhere else.)

But, exhaustion or not, you're in a battle to bring life to your novel.

# DAY 7: RIP THE RUG OUT

## WISK

*"Want some candy? Tempting, but I'm waiting for a lull in the action. That's what a lull is, candy. Mmm, sweet."* - Steve Windsor

## What You'll Learn

Day 7 - Part 3: Reaction to Second Pinch to Second Plot Point

- All these evil forces running around. It's gotta exhaust the hero at some point. It's going to tire the reader out a little too.
- In this section, we'll talk about how to let everyone take a big breath of fresh air—right after they react to the Second Pinch Point.
- We'll talk about how to use a lull right before the Second Plot Point to deliver a little tiny tidbit of information to your audience. At the same time the lull will give them a brief instant to relax . . . right before you rip the rug out from under their world again.
- The lull conveys something your reader needs to understand—a piece of your puzzle they may not yet have figured out. It's going to hint at the Second Plot Point, but not spoil

it. So when the Second Plot Point comes, everyone will open their eyes up wider than the first. Another "OMG" moment.

## Been There, Done That

Now we're into plot spoiler territory, so if you don't want to do that and you want to read my books, skip this.

In *FURY*, I battled that angel through her own resurrection, trials, and redemption through Parts 1, 2 and 3, and by the time she got to the Second Plot Point, she'd been kidnapped, beaten, raped, and was now so angry that she wanted nothing more than revenge and killing.

And just when that was about to be delivered into her hands, I revealed to her via her father-figure angel friend that if she did take revenge on the one responsible, she could never again be with the love of her life—which happened to be part of the point and goal of her entire journey back to the Garden.

Revenge inches away . . . and not a drop of blood to spill.

## Nail on the Head

As a subplot point two, I revealed that Fury's real father was actually someone she'd killed in the past and would have to kill again in the future.

During the process of revealing the Second Plot Point—the real world your hero had no idea about even after the First Plot Point—you're going to deliver everything the hero now needs to be able to fight back and win in Part 4.

After the end of Part 3, you're not supposed to introduce any new information, though I haven't seen a plot twist ending or series cliffhanger yet that didn't break this "rule" at least a little. Deus ex machina? Take that with a grain of salt.

In *FURY*, I did this at a few points on the way to the final battle scene. There's nothing like whipping open a literal door and seeing two million demonic angels of Armageddon waiting for you, making your entire journey, revelation, and resolve to win appear moot.

## Ticking clock

And finally, there has to be some type of time limit to everything in your story. A ticking clock, if you will. The race against time is so universally done and recognized that many stories have simply forgone hinting at it and inserted a literal ticking clock in the form of a time bomb or actual clock, or the hero continually asking someone, "How much time do we have?"

In the movie *RUN LOLA RUN* – Franka Potente has 20

minutes to deliver 100,000 German marks to save her boyfriend. She keeps repeating the events over and over until she does. It's a great example of the ticking clock. Check it out.

## Reaction to Second Pinch Point

As for our fictitious romance hero's reaction to the news that his daughter ran into the marine mammal ex-guy . . . well, by now he's most likely had enough of that guy messing up his world. He's going to have to do something.

Storm out of dinner, go find the guy, yell at him, punch him, tell him to stay away from his family—something . . . something stupid . . . that's doomed to fail or at least make our hero look bad in everyone's eyes. All the while he doesn't even know the real reason why he should be doing that. He thinks it's impending divorce.

## Pre-Second Plot Point Lull

And in the lull, we may see Wifey thumbing through old photos of high school and finding one of her and her ex-guy. And then maybe she just glances at a picture of her entire family on her dresser—the one of her husband and two daughters.

But maybe she focuses in a little too much on one of her

daughters. The one who doesn't quite look like her other daughter . . . or husband. The daughter telling the story at dinner. The 20-year-old who just happens to look an awful lot like marine mammal ex-guy!

## Lead up to Second Plot Point

Now, Wifey isn't frantic—she knows. Hero doesn't know, but she does. This can only train-wreck from here. And what we want is for the reader to see the blown-out bridge ahead and fear for our hero, but know there's nothing to be done. He's going to plummet into the chasm of the canyon.

But what no one knows, including our reader, is that we're going to put alligators in the river down at the bottom of that canyon . . . just in case any of them survives the train wreck that's coming.

Now, all we have to do is get them all together—Wifey, hero, daughter, marine mammal ex-guy, and maybe hero's drinking buddy for good sport and to urge the hero to fight back.

This is where the lead up to the second plot point comes in. We may see twentysomething daughter bump into marine mammal ex-guy again and invite him to dinner, because he says he used to know her mom. Or maybe it's something else that happened before when they met the first time that none of us saw.

Wifey craps when she hears that daughter invited marine mammal ex-guy, and she starts primping to get herself presentable for dinner, and daughter is disgusted with her. And when our hero finds out, he gets angry and storms out of the house to his drinking buddy's. And now the stage is set.

Guess who's coming to dinner!

**Second Plot Point**

The world changes again . . . forever.

Keep in mind that when you start writing the Second Plot Point scenes, you just want to let your mind run wild with evil little thoughts, just like mine is doing right now. Because that's the good stuff. When your fingers can't keep up with the action, but you're giddy at the prospect of the Jerry Springer episode you just set up for dinner, you're on the right track.

In our little story, we may choose to slowly show everyone arriving and let the tension build and build until it's like an overfilled balloon that you know has to pop. That's Tarantino style and he's a master at it.

In fact, watch the basement bar scene in *Inglourious*

*Basterds*. It's a tension-building powder keg of anticipation that starts off with Brad Pitt staring across the street at the lit-up window of a basement, spouting lines like, "You've got us fighting in a basement?" In the audience, we know the train wreck is coming. If you can do that, you've got it made. Or. . .

We may choose to bury the reader deep in the scene—everyone already at the dinner table and the glances and looks and confusion is building. And once you have everyone at dinner jumping out of their seats and your reader thinking they have a complete handle on what's going to happen, you're going to unleash . . . the alligators.

**Deliver the unthinkable.**

As it turns out, our hero's adventurous older daughter, who has never displayed any of the genetic predispositions that daddy has and Wifey knows why . . . has been invited to go back to Borneo with marine mammal ex-guy and study his . . . ahem . . . "laser sharks."

I can feel your "Oh, that's just gross!" in the background, but marine mammal guy also had no idea that the little escapade he had with Wifey two days before he left for Borneo, when Wifey got engaged to our hero 20 years ago, produced hero's older "daughter." But wait, it gets worse.

Because all this time, disgruntled with her life, Wifey wanted to try and rekindle with marine mammal ex-guy, and now her daughter, who is his daughter too, is going to Borneo? Not happening! "Yeah, not happening!" (That's our hero.)

Because now, Wifey and hero have something to come back together over. Marine mammal guy is too old for their precious daughter, not to frickin' mention that she's actually marine mammal ex-guy's *daughter* and that would be just . . . sick.

So, hero is pissed, but Wifey is sickened and pissed. And so are you and so is the reader. And that's why they're still reading.

A nice sit-down dinner with old exes is no fun at all. But a dinner explosion? Heck yeah!

Now here's where things can get crazy: If you're not careful, you won't realize that as fast as you reveal plot point two, your characters will go nuts racing for the angry safety of kicking ass and taking names in Part 4 of your story—wanting to skip right over "hero accepts reality" scenes on their way to pent-up vindication and revenge.

And we don't have far to go before our little romantic story turns into an all-out cat-and-dog fight. Just a little bit more.

Our hero's drinking buddy guy starts laughing at him and then teases him. Now our hero is steaming, but he's civilized so he's not actually gonna go all kung fu on marine mammal real daddy (something neither hero nor real daddy know yet) just yet. He needs a little push. Come to think of it, so does Wifey.

So in order to bond hero and Wifey back together in the New Equilibrium—after the climax battle scene—we're going to have to give them something to weld them back together or drive a spike right between them. Assuming we want them back together in some sort of satisfying "everything worked out" ending, that is.

## Revealing the Second Plot Point

In Wifey's mind, there's just no way that her daughter is going to Borneo with her own father that she doesn't even know is her father to—unthinkable. But she can see that look in her rebellious daughter's eyes and she knows what it means—the girl's smitten already.

Now all thoughts in Wifey's mind about rekindling with marine mammal ex-guy have turned to angry mother protection for her daughter. She doesn't want to sleep with marine mammal ex-guy—she thought she did, but not now—and she'll be damned if marine mammal guy is going to—but it's too late for that and here we go!

## Ticking Clock

Confrontation ensues in our little romance train wreck and marine mammal ex-guy says they're all nuts. He announces that he has to fly back to Borneo in . . . whatever, two hours. Now, daughter knew that and she has a plane ticket to go with him. Holy crap!

Marine mammal ex-guy tells "daughter" if she still wants to go with him, she has his number. Exit stage left for the villain.

## Ticking Clock Purpose and Position

In reality, you can put the Ticking Clock anywhere, including right up front in Part 1. It drives everyone to the end under a time limit. That's its job. *Die Hard*—gotta diffuse the bomb!

I like Larry Brooks' positioning of it at the Second Plot Point, because you spring something unbelievable on the hero, and then give him or her an almost unachievable time limit to fix it.

The ticking clock gives urgency to our hero and his plight. It has to be solved, yes, but it also has to be solved within a certain amount of time or he will fail—his "stakes" will be lost forever.

And that's why the end of any good story races to a proverbial finish line.

**Back to our "romance."**

As it turns out, daughter informs them all that she and marine mammal ex-guy already did it in the bathroom of the diner where they "bumped" into each other and it was awesome! And she's going to Borneo in spite of the silly protests of her boring parents. "I'm 20, I'm going!"

Ouch! And Yuck!

And now . . . you know you wanna turn this page and find out. You want to know if Wifey comes clean, goes nuts, or runs. You want to know if hero will chase down marine mammal ex-guy, cry, slap, yell, scream. . . And so does your audience. People love watching train wrecks.

I sure want to find out, because though I wrote an entire outline of the 4PSS, as long as I'm hitting all the points I need to, I'm free to improvise along the way.

And that little tidbit to you is just about the best Second Plot Point double entendre I can give you. Because we're about three quarters through this book and I've been hounding you about structure-structure-structure, write-write-write. And now I go and tell you that the outline you wrote is just a guide?

You've got to be kidding me! Unthinkable! . . . Exactly.

## Multiple Revelations

The machine gun Second Plot Point(s)

When you rip a rug out from under your hero, you may have several rugs ripping out at once. In our romance saga, we do.

Daughter's revelation that she already did the deed with marine mammal ex-guy hits our hero hard, but think about what it does to Wifey.

Daughter storms out, the clock is ticking, she's going to Borneo. And she's out the door before Wifey has time to tell daughter the truth. Air sucks out of the room and now all that's left is steaming panicked Wifey, mad hero, and, with mouth open almost laughing, hero's buddy.

Since we don't want Wifey more crazed than our hero . . . she has to come clean. If we want our hero really steamed, we leave his buddy in the room.

Scene: Wifey reveals to hero that they can't let daughter get on plane with marine mammal ex-guy because . . . daughter is actually marine mammal's daughter! They have less than two hours to stop daughter and they don't know where either of them are. No time for hero to get angry with Wifey.

In fact, it may be that hero's buddy already knew about it from way back when. In fact, it may be that the whole damn town knew and hero is such a good guy that no one had the heart to tell him. But hero has to stop daughter, deal with Wifey later.

If we want it *really* crazy, Wifey has to drive she and hero to the airport because hero lost his license because of driving while intoxicated incident way back in Part 2 (remember). That trip will not be fun.

## Examples of "Unthinkable" Plot Reveals

Let's pause. If you don't believe this storyline—think it's just implausible and would never work, sell, or be accepted by a publishing house, take a look at these examples:

*Me, Myself, and Irene* - Jim Carey's character's wife has three African American babies with "him." He's in denial that she has slept with their short, African American limousine driver and he snaps into a tough brute, beating up anyone in his path.

*Guess Who's Coming to Dinner* - Spencer Tracy. A classic. And at the time, an African American man marrying a white woman was unthinkable.

*Something's Gotta Give* - Jack Nicholson's character sleeps with the daughter of a woman that he eventually falls in love with and sleeps with, but can't quite give up his cradle-robbing to admit it to her or himself.

He finally accepts that he's in love with Diane Keaton, flies to Paris and . . . snap, she's on date with young doctor guy Keanu Reeves.

## My All-Time Favorite Second Plot Point Reveal
*Lone Star* - Matthew McConaughey and Chris Cooper. I hesitate to spoil this for you, but you should definitely watch it for the second plot point reveal alone.

The plot actually keeps you so distracted from the hero's second plot point revelation, that when the rug is ripped out, you'll scrunch up your face and go, "OMG—eww!"

One of my favorite lines from *Lone Star* is such a wonderful use of foreshadowing that I may have to go back and put this in the foreshadowing chapter. (I just did, but I did that a long time ago as far as you know. Time travel, it exists in novels.) Like I said, you want your reader to have revelations as they read as well.

The *Lone Star* foreshadow that led up to the second plot point reveal went like this:

Wesley Birdsong, an Indian that our hero is pumping for information about his father, hands our hero a big dead rattlesnake.

"Here... This big fella was sleeping in a crate at Cisco's junkyard. Right when **I was gonna open to see what was in her**. Jumped right at my face. Scared me so bad I had to **kill him without thinking**. **Gotta be careful where you go pokin'. Who knows what you'll find**."

All of those bold parts are direct, literal reveals later in the movie. I didn't even realize some of them until I went back and read it right now!

And when the *Lone Star* hero finally finds his answer, he gets bitten so bad by it, that a rattlesnake might as well have sunk its fangs into his neck and filled him up with venom.

And that's what we want to happen to our romance hero.

**Tips, Tools and Time**

Right about now, I have to pause, because I want you to just feel something. . . Feel that? If you do, then I did what is the entire point of this whole book: I sucked you in. If not, then figure out what would have sucked you in—what would have gotten your blood boiling—and that's what you're going to put into your story at this point.

That goes into your outline for a Second Plot Point.

And I don't care if Wifey chases marine mammal guy to airport to confront him, but ends up having sex with him in a bathroom (foreshadowing) and then tells him that daughter girl is *his* daughter.

Or if hero bursts in on Wifey and mammal guy and kills them both. Or if hero, Wifey, and marine mammal guy decide to wife-share back and forth from Borneo or whatever it is.

What it has to do is make someone yell at their screen or page, "No, you can't do that, or that's so wrong, or OMG, no way!"

As an author, you need reactions. You'll get good ones and bad ones, but you need them and want them.

Indifference is the killer.

You wanna find out what hero does to marine mammal ex-guy? I thought so, but we're done with this chapter.

**TTOTD**

Right about now, you and your hero are going to be so

pumped up that you won't need motivation to write, you won't need inspiration to write, you won't even need a place to write. You'll just need time. Because here's where the beauty of writing your story is all coming together. You're racing right along with your hero, chasing the words with your fingers. Your job as an author is to simply make sure you keep up.

Keep your laptop, assuming that's what you write on, close at hand at all times. Though I preach big blocks of time, there will be moments—10, 20, 30-minute breaks in life—that you'll have inspiration and opportunity to write, and the climax scenes are some of the classic times that inspiration and perspiration meet to make crazy word counts happen.

I'm talking 1,500 to 2,000 an hour!

While I wait to pick up my kids at school, my laptop is out and I'm tapping as fast as I can for the 15 minutes until the literal "ticking clock" of the school bell rings and I have to slam it shut and race to their classes to get them.

## :: Action Steps for Day 7

- Write your hero's reaction to the Second Pinch Point—the reintroduction of the evil force.
- Write the lull—give your reader a little tidbit of useful information, but don't spoil the Sec-

ond Plot Point.
- Unleash your rug-ripping Second Plot Point and force your reader and your hero to freak out when they read it.
- Our word goal for "Day" 8 is 5,000-10,000.
- So block out the time: 5-10 hours.

## 10K A DAY Strategy

### The **"Barely Legal"**

18 days straight of five-hour nights.

It can be done. I've done it. And at 1,000 words an hour, that's 90,000 words in 18 days.

Full-length novel done in a little over half a month!

## 5K A DAY Strategy

The Bay Area is famous for two-hour commutes. I've done them. One thing you can do is grab the application "Dragon Dictate" for your mobile and dictate your novel while you commute.

I've done it. Takes your brain a little getting used to, but once you're in it, you come up to speed fast.

I won't say it's one-for-one to typing time, but you could

get 50% efficiency on your time-wasting commute.

So, two hours there and then your three hours at night. Five hours done.

# DAY 8: CLIMAX BATTLE

## WISK

*"Wow, that Second Plot Point was disgusting. Both of them really ripped the rug out from under me. How do you think that stuff up? . . . And now you're on your back. Where to go from there?"* - Steve Windsor

## What You'll Learn

- Day 8 - Part 4: Second Plot Point through Climax
- So we've ripped the wool off of our hero's eyes, made him run for his life, given him the understanding and courage to try and fight back a little, and then we ripped the rug right out from under his feet again. Now all he has to do is . . . save the day.
- In this part you'll learn why you've never seen a movie ending where the hero didn't almost die right before he overcame the bad guy.
- And you'll also see why some people say that Four Part Story Structure needs to play out like good sex.

## Been There, Done That

In *FAITH*, I started my ticking clock at the beginning of the book. My hero had to save a "dead" angel and I gave him one eternal "day" to do it.

Throughout the entire story, I send challenge after challenge at him that he can still overcome, but every instance he loses time—the one thing that's running out.

When I pull the covers back on what he has to do to save his angel, I throw a fire-breathing demon at him to fight. And he has only one hour left and a 30-minute run through the city to get back to his primary task. But do I let him defeat that demon easily? No. I can't, you can't, no one can.

If you've run your hero hard enough through his own story, by the end we have to know that he barely has the ability, much less the energy, left to win. In the final battle scene or climax, he or she has to have some mini try-and-fail moments.

In fact, the battle scenes in the climax are a mini 4PSS in and of themselves.

**Here's an example of what I mean:**
- Our hero shows up at the dripping, abandoned warehouse that the witch villain told him to retrieve his love. (PART 1 - Setup)

- Witch pops out . . . with five witch friends. OMG! (First Plot Point)
- Battle begins and hero is pummeled near-senseless by witches. (PART 2 - Run for your life!)
- Hero realizes that some of the witches are harmed by water. Hero now understands he can use water to defeat witches and he has renewed energy to fight. (PART 2 - Figure out)
- (PART 3 - Fight back with a plan, but lose) Hero fights back with water, secondary witches are killed, but main witch is impervious to water! (PART 3 of Climax scenes - Plot Point 2)
- As they tussle, hero sees main witch get burned by hot pipe in warehouse. (PART 4 - Hero understands)
- Hero pulls out lighter and tries to set witch on fire. Witch defends and slams hero to almost to death. (PART 4 - Battle Scene)
- Witch leans over hero to gloat and monologue. (All villains like to monologue before they kill a hero.) Hero plays dead and then grabs witch by her cloak and sets her on fire. Witch goes up in flames. (PART 4 - Climax)
- Hero lies on ground and breaths breathes hard, totally spent but safe. (PART 4 New equilibrium)

That's why in any action movie you've ever watched, when you think the villain goes down too quickly, he or she actually does.

A Villain always, always, always comes back from an apparent easy defeat, to give the hero one last ass-whooping before the hero can somehow miraculously defeat him or her.

When the hero finally does—finally beats the clock—he or she has to collapse, exhausted and completely spent, but victorious. Just like great sex. Or so "they" say.

**Nail on the Head**

By the time we get to the climax scenes, the roller coaster we will have taken our hero and reader on should have been so exciting, so up, down and all-around exhausting, that they can barely finish.

By the climax scenes, if you're writing as fast as you can, you should be as exhausted as your hero.

**Why some people compare 4PSS to great sex:**
- Slowly introduce all the wonderful world our hero lives in, see all the tight clothes and beautiful bodies. (Part 1 - Setup)
- Then someone says, "I love you" too soon. (First Plot Point)

- Then the hero stops the intimacy and leaves. (Part 2 - run for your life.)
- Then h Hero slowly understands what he or she is up against—maybe their own feelings about the other person. (End of Part 2—mid-point—figure out)
- Then—surprise!—we're back in the bedroom with our hero and his love. (Part 3 - fight back—lose)
- Hot and heavy and BAM! Hero's love is pregnant from another guy? Or girl hero has to reveal that. (Second Plot Point - end of Part 3)
- Hero understands what he's up against and loves/lusts for love anyway. Hero has to accept another man's child in order to be with love of his life. (Part 4 - hero accepts)
- The "battle" scenes ensue and then "climax." (Part 4 - Climax)
- Then hero and partner lie in bed exhausted from best they've ever had because they're in love.
- Flash to them getting married, girl is noticeably pregnant, and holding hand of baby number one. (Second Plot Point - baby. And that's Part 4 - new equilibrium)

Bravo!

Pop champagne!

Call editor. . .

## Hero Accepts Reality of Situation

Back to our romance, because I want to know what happens.

Now we have hero, Wifey, and hero's buddy in dining room. Air sucked out of room. (Part 4 - Hero Accepts - Calm before the storm)

Now hero understands everything and has to accept that daughter is not his, but he has to stop her from leaving with marine mammal ex-guy. He'll deal with Wifey later, or maybe at same time. Our hero storms out after daughter. (We won't do the car scene.)

Wifey looks at hero's drinking buddy. "I told you to tell him years ago," says drinking buddy guy. Wifey, feeling guilty, storms out. Hero's buddy sits back down and pours himself some more wine. No need for him to get burned by all this. If daughter needs consoling afterward, he'll "help" out with that. (That's how single drinking buddy guys are —"helpful.")

## Climax Battle Scene

Our romance battle scene will be, you guessed it, at the airport! How many times have you seen heroes race through airports that are now impenetrable fortresses due to the new terrorist procedures?

No one is rushing to gates in the new world we live in. But this is fiction—**suspension of disbelief**—not the book for that.

Back to our hero!

Hero storms through security on way to finding daughter. Maybe he catches daughter and marine mammal ex-guy kissing and slugs him. Then marine mammal ex, in shape, pummels hero.

Our hero isn't fighting, in this case, so much to beat marine mammal guy as he is fighting himself to determine if he wants his wife/marriage back. The act of fighting with marine mammal guy may signify the decision to take back what he let go in the first place, his "give a shit."

Daughter screaming, Wifey shows up and screams at hero. She screams at marine mammal guy, too, and he craps his pants that he has a daughter. Daughter stands dumbfounded, too—she slept with her *father*? Holy shit! Marine mammal guy stands dumbfounded and guilty, though not entirely through fault of his own.

Hero stands up and pummels marine mammal guy with sucker punch. Marine mammal guy out cold. Hero yells at Wifey for hiding truth from him. Wifey has no defense.

Hero leaves airport with arm around crying daughter girl.

Wifey stands over slowly reawakening marine mammal guy. She's disgusted and feeling guilty, he's disgusted and feeling guilty—they're the bad guys—they're defeated.

On to the New Equilibrium.

## A Quick Example

Once again—conflict, conflict, conflict. And if you still think our little made-up romance storyline isn't plausible, watch the movie *Love Actually*.

With so many character stories racing towards the end in that movie, it's a great example of multiple plots tied to one another, all racing toward the end.

One of them ends up—you guessed it—at the airport, "almost missed the plane" love scene. Not to mention middle-aged man cheats on wife, wife discovers it at Christmas, confronts husband at their child's Christmas play, and he's hammered in final battle that lasts a few seconds. Wife sticks up for herself and asks him what he would do if tables were turned.

Final battles don't have to be bloody. But someone's getting injured.

## Tips, Tools and Time

After writing this book in less than two full 10-hour days, guess what? Deep into the beginning of Part 4 of this book, I'm exhausted.

Metaphor, simile, hyperbole, double entendre all wrapped into one. I think.

I can tell you this: Having a great 4PSS outline helps at this point, because once you write the battle scene, you'll be emotionally and physically spent.

It will be hard to motivate yourself to finish your story/ novel. The New Equilibrium scenes will seem trite and common to you. You'll want to just close the scene after hero defeats nemesis and be done with it.

Don't do that!

We'll talk in the next chapter about New Equilibrium scenes and their importance. For now, take a deep breath. Your hero has won!

## TTOTD

Fully charge your computer every day before you leave for the day. There's nothing more annoying than being in the middle of some great writing when your laptop runs out of power.

I write at coffeehouses . . . a lot. Cliche, I realize, but I like the background noise. For some reason it helps me drown things out. Or maybe it's just where they keep the caffeine. Jury's out on that.

It also happens to be where they keep the power. Yet, when it's crowded, I can't get close enough to plug in. Small tip, I realize, but worth searing into your mind.

## :: Action Steps for Day 8

- Write the hero accepting the reality of his or her situation. Steel the hero's resolve to fight back and win.
- Write the climax battle scene, but be careful not to let your hero triumph too easily. Make him or her struggle through the entire 4PSS inside-the-climax battle scene as well.
- If you do that, you can get a lot of word count out of a section that tempts you to just defeat the bad guy too quickly.
- Our word goal for "Day" 9 is 5,000-10,000.
- So block out the time: 5-10 hours.

## 10K A DAY Strategy

## The "No Tell Motel"

If you're writing a murder mystery, or a thriller, or a love story where someone cheats on someone else at one of those seedy motels, wouldn't it be nice to be able to describe what that place was like? . . . From first-hand experience?

I know you're scared, I know they're gross, and I know you can't sleep there because of all of the nightly . . . "activity" going on. However. . .

You want to know *how* I know? Because I've been there, done that.

No, no! To write, not that! Okay . . . maybe once.

Anyway, check into a seedy motel for an extended week. It'll cost you about $300 and you'll have more uninterrupted time and material after that than any research will ever give you. Because this *is* research.

You know what else you'll have? You'll have another novel written!

## 5K A DAY Strategy

Sick days. I know, I know, but I've had sick days where it was simply important for me not to be around other humans to give them the cold. That didn't mean I was incapacitated.

And since I actually *like* to write, it keeps my mind off of my cold and makes me feel better.

# DAY 9: NEW EQUILIBRIUM

## WISK

*"That was awesome! What? I just clim—don't even say it. By the way, you wanna get married?"* - Steve Windsor

## What You'll Learn

- Day 9 - Part 4: Climax Battle Scene through Resolution
- You'll learn why easing your hero and reader out of the climax and into their new world is important.
- You'll learn how to use a New Equilibrium section to fulfill your reader's need for a satisfying ending.
- And you'll learn how to drop in a cliffhanger at the end of the New Equilibrium to set up your next book, episode, or installment.

You knew you were writing another novel, right?

## Been There, Done That

I love my *Fallen* series characters so much, that by the time each of my anti-heroes "wins" in the climax battle scene, I'm spent from typing so hard and so fast that I hesitate to write the New Equilibrium.

So I take a break.

What? Steve, you said race-race-race? Okay, yes, but here, in order to make a great transition from all hell breaking loose—death, destruction and mayhem—what we want to do is be in the same mindset as the scenes we're about to write.

So I take a break. Maybe it's 30 minutes, maybe it's 10, or a day or whatever. But step away from the adrenaline rush of the Part 4 battle scenes and let you and your hero's worlds slow down.

I do it to switch gears from blood and bullies and get to happily never after. They're different mindsets and places for your hero and you need to feel differently to write them.

## Nail on the Head

In a Western, the hero rides into the sunset. In a Romance, the lovers get married at a big wedding. In an action movie, some actor—twice the age of the love interest—drives away from the bloody carnage with his cradle-robbed damsel or unlikely sidekick holding his gun. In a Fantasy, they all sit around in a laughing-and-loud pub, drinking grog from wooden mugs, slapping bosom-bursting maidens on the bum.

These are all New Equilibrium scenes that give the reader satisfaction and closure.

## New Equilibrium

One thing audiences and readers hate is not knowing what happened to their wonderful heroes after they've defeated evil or successfully completed their quest.

Readers want to lie in bed naked next to their new hero and revel in their wonderful new world.

I'm mixing analogies here. Just go with it.

So, what you have to give them is a wondrous New Equilibrium to wallow in and smile at.

This is what the scenes after the Climax are for, especially in a series as you also get to introduce the cliffhanger that will make your audience want to read your next story or episode or season two.

## Don't cheat the New Equilibrium scenes.

If you like sugary endings, give your hero everything he or she ever wanted.

After all, novels are entertainment to distract and delight

us from the challenges of everyday life. We want them to give us what we don't get each day—victory and its spoils.

If you're evil and mischievous like me, give your hero exactly what he or she wants, but make them pay such a heavy toll that they wonder if it was worth it.

Or if your theme is one of futility, make the victory an actual defeat to prove your point. Though, more and more, I'm coming to the conclusion that people just want the candy and not more to think about.

Dead hero martyrs—*not* an audience favorite.

**Our Own Little Story. . .**

Hero dad guy and daughter girl leave and hero consoles daughter that mother still loves her but wants divorce from hero dad.

At this point, our hero may or may not care if he salvages marriage with Wifey. His revenge may be to let marine mammal guy break her heart all over again. However, he can't lose children in divorce. So, we don't let him.

Flash forward a couple months: Wifey lives in Borneo with not-so-hot marine mammal guy, but hero dad lives with two daughters who chose to stay with him instead of lying, conniving Wifey. And now hero dad guy has hot new girlfriend who paints nails and gossips/shops with hero guy's daughters.

Hero dad has lost weight, won the lottery (hey, it's fiction), and has a new hot future Wifey.

Sure, daughter girl is in therapy for the "daddy" incident, but hero dad and new mommy/girlfriend/mother figure/friend is helping her cope.

And hero guy's single drinking buddy? He knocked up a waitress at their favorite bar with twins and he has to get married because her dad is the sheriff.

After I wrote this, I related the story to my wife and she was disgusted, which I liked, but she said, "Marine mammal guy can't end up with anyone, he's sick!"

That just goes to show you that even an unwitting villain will elicit a visceral response from your reader if he's involved in something bad enough.

## Cliffhangers

The purpose of this book was to give you inspiration to write one fiction novel very quickly and introduce you to the tools and methods that could help you do that.

However, one of the most important reasons to write efficiently and fast is so you can write another novel.

In order to smoothly transition to our next story in a series, we have to leave something for our hero to have to clean up. Some loose end they have to deal with. An evil force that's still out there, lurking. Readers love and hate this, so it's delicate.

Maybe in our romance story, daughter is secretly, unknowingly showing signs of something. Maybe at the end of our happy New Equilibrium, our hero's hot new girlfriend/mommy figure catches 20-year-old daughter throwing up in the bathroom the very next morning.

Uh-oh! Snap, snap, snap!

**Tips, Tools and Time**

**TTOTD**

At the end of your novel, if it's a series, you'll have momentum and ideas swirling around in your mind. Especially if you leave a tantalizing cliffhanger at the end.

Rather than put everything down to take a breath—conventional wisdom—hammer out a few ideas in rapid succession about what your next novel might look like.

The ideas are fresh in your mind, you're coming off of a big win, and there's no time like the present.

I find myself blasting into the beginning of my next novel in *The Fallen*, because I have purposefully made the reader want to know more about that character in the book before. I'll write a quick opening scene of 1,000 words to give myself a placeholder to come back to.

And that's the value of the 4PSS overlaid into the series: I know what I have to set up by the end of the current novel.

## :: Action Steps for Day 9

- Take a small break to transition from Climax to writing New Equilibrium scenes.
- Give your hero everything he or she wants in New Equilibrium scenes, or martyr him or her. Different, but both valid endings.
- If you're writing a series, introduce a cliffhanger antagonistic force at the very last scene to beg your readers to come back for the next book, episode, season.

## 10K A DAY Strategy

This is my favorite, because it throws the world into a panic. I love that.

## "What Happens in Vegas"

Don't ask permission to go. Don't tell anyone where you're going. And just go . . . somewhere . . . else.

Escape to a place where your everyday, time-killing, minutia-filled, hour-busting life can't rob you of your hours to write.

This works much better when you're single with no kids, as otherwise it can have negative side effects when you get back. But it *is* effective and you *will* write your novel. And when you get back, I can guarantee one of two things—both good from a writer/author perspective:

One, if you're single, the world will have kept spinning, the sun will have kept shining, the TV news will still be more of the same, and they will have invented a new reality TV show to suck your brain cells out once and for all. And you know what? . . . They'll have done it all without you. But *you* will have the draft of your novel.

Two, if you're married, involved, have a S.O., or have kids —and doctors, don't try to get in here and spoil this, because in an emergency, there's always a doctor somewhere. . .

Anyway, at the end of this all, when you get back, there will be such an emotional upheaval that you'll have a new novel and an entire explosive plot for the next one.

Think about it—hero disappears, spouse has him/her declared legally dead in nine days, hero confused and bewildered, hero's buddy is now living with hero's hot race-car-driver wife.

Hero's drunk dad comes back from being missing to teach hero how to get back his mojo, hero saves day to a new, better beginning.

Crazy? Not even. *Talladega Nights: The Ballad Of Ricky Bobby*

## 5K A DAY Strategy

I'll close out this section by saying that—at least in America—for some reason we've gone out of our way to invent more and more ways to celebrate nothing.

We have a day off for everything. What we don't get in annual vacation, we make up for in three-day weekends and meaningless holidays invented by greeting card stores.

Instead of that next Oscar celebration party, watching the pompous primp each other, use those days to write.

And here's an idea: If you're serious about writing, then

that's what you want for your birthday—time to write.

I know that's what I'm asking for on mine.

# WORD COUNT

**WISK**

*"That was like, 169,945 strokes . . . of the keyboard. You were counting? I always count."* - Steve Windsor

Actually Scrivener counts the words for me. [shameless plug]

**Word Count**

This will be my final rant about word count and whether or not this *Nine Day Novel* book is valid for you, or whether the steps and motivation in it will work.

I started this book . . . yesterday at 6:00 AM.

After I paused and made breakfast for my wife and kids, she took our kids to school, and I wrote from 7:00 AM to 2:15 PM. Then I picked my kids up from school at 2:50 PM and got back home at 3:30 PM.

My two daughters and I went on a 30-minute hike, I made them dinner, helped them with homework, and then they read while I wrote again from 5:30 PM to about 7:00 PM when my wife got home.

Dinner, chit-chat, teeth brushing, herding a six- and eight-year-old to bed and story time (imagine what that's like at an angry religious thriller author's house), and then I wrote from about 9:00 PM to about 11:30 PM and then passed out at about 12:00 midnight.

About 10 hours of writing.

This morning, I got up, brushed teeth, got coffee, and started writing again at 6:30 AM. It's now 3:30 PM and I've typed probably all but about 30 minutes of that.

About eight and a half hours. I love math. 18-19 hours into this draft, I have roughly 20,000 words (at the end 30,000).

That's a little better than my good pace of 1,000 per hour. And I skimmed back through it a little, cheating. It's not all crap, which is just a self-critical author's way of saying it can be edited into a decent book (which is where my partner, Lise, comes in). Maybe even a good book.

Marathon sprints. They work for me.

I hope I've persuaded you to at least *try* one. They sure beat waiting for six months to find out if my hero husband is going to kick marine mammal ex-guy's ass.

You *can* write a novel in nine days. I know you can.

# NEXT STEPS

## What's Next?

Now what did I say about the New Equilibrium?

I took a break and I'm writing this section a day after finishing the daily writing sections.

So in our new world, you have been inundated with the Four Part Story Structure, its sections, and those section's purposes. You've also seen examples, both big and small, seemingly ludicrous and totally, beautifully unthinkable.

What now?

Well, if you made it all the way to the end of this book, congratulations! I know how I write—I throw a lot at you, very quickly. I hope you get a lot out of it. I know I learned even more writing and researching it, and I reinforced some things I had forgotten.

So take a break.

As authors, especially we yet-to-be-millionaire authors,

we tend to want to jump back into the pool and start swimming hard again.

Take a little break, have a drink, and smile. You wrote a novel, maybe even in nine days! That is so sweet!

Congratulations!

## JOIN ME

I encourage you to **follow my progress as an author and get access to awesome tools** and how-to guides to use on your own author journey.

To entice you, Lise Cartwright and I wrote a free book for you, *29 Truths From the Trenches of Self-Publishing*.

You can get that book and get notified when our new authorship books come out, by clicking HERE. You can also visit http://authorbasics.com/lp1.

**You can reach me here:**
Email: steve@authorbasics.com

**Other author how-to books in the *Nine Day Novel* series:**

9 Day Novel: Authorphobia
9 Day Novel: Outlining
9 Day Novel: Writing
9 Day Novel: Self-Editing
9 Day Novel: Self-Publishing
9 Day Novel: Book Marketing
9 Day Novel: Writing a Series

# ABOUT THE AUTHOR

**ABOUT THE AUTHOR**

Steve Windsor was born in Augsburg, Germany to U.S. military parents. So he doesn't know a bit of German.

I'm just a guy who decided to write one day. And roughly two years and two million words into it, I've learned so much and my writing has improved so much. . . But it all came at a cost in time and frustration. I've bled words.

My belief is that I have information you need to avoid some of the frustration and pain that I suffered in starting up my dream. And simply put, I want to write books for you because of it.

The fiction I write is hard and raw and my non-fiction is even harder. I don't like to mince words.

I like heroes and villains just about the same, because a good villain usually has a bad backstory that isn't really his or her fault. Sure you gotta kill them, but realize you're going to be a little sad about it, too.

I'm here to help you grow as an author. The best way you can do that—go write something!

— Steve Windsor
Best-Selling Author & Writing Coach

# I Need your help!

Thank you for reading this book!
I'd love to get your input so I can make the next book in
the *Nine Day Novel* series even better.
I'll have my personal chauffeur, Novella, drive you over
to Amazon so you can leave a helpful review, letting me
know what you thought of the book.
Click HERE and fasten your seatbelt.
She's a wild driver!
Thanks so much!

Made in the USA
San Bernardino, CA
17 April 2019